A

CU

FOR THE

EARLY YEARS

Edited by

Angela Anning

Open University Press
Buckingham · Philadelphia

Open University Press
Celtic Court
22 Ballmoor
Buckingham
MK18 1XW

and

1900 Frost Road, Suite 101
Bristol, PA 19007, USA

First Published 1995

A catalogue record of this book is available from the British Library

ISBN   0 335 19431 1 (pb)   0 335 19432 X (hb)

Library of Congress Cataloging-in-Publication Data
A national curriculum for the early years / edited by Angela Anning.
       p.   cm.
    Continues: The first years at school / Angela Anning.
    Includes bibliographical references and index.
    ISBN 0-335-19432-X. (hb) ISBN 0-335-19431-1 (pb)
       1. Early childhood education—Great Britain—Curricula. 2.
Education. Preschool—Great Britain—Curricula. I. Anning, Angela.
1944–   . II. Anning, Angela, 1944–   First years at school.
LB1139.4.N38 1995
372.19—dc20   95-10789
                                                                  CIP

Typeset by Type Study, Scarborough
Printed in Great Britain by St Edmundsbury Press Ltd
Bury St Edmunds, Suffolk

CONTENTS

For all the Key Stage One teachers who struggled to manage the unmanageable

LIST OF
CONTRIBUTORS

Angela Anning is Senior Lecturer in Primary Education (Arts and Early Years) for the School of Education at the University of Leeds. She is the author of many articles on primary education and Early Years education and *The First Years at School* (1991). Her research interests are Art and Technology education in primary schools and teachers' professional knowledge.

Hilary Asoko is Lecturer (Science) for the School of Education at the University of Leeds. Her research interests are the development of teaching strategies designed to promote more effective conceptual understanding of science, with particular emphasis on the primary classroom, and the professional development of teachers. She has written amongst other things (with P. Scott, R. Driver and J. Emberton) Working from children's ideas: an analysis of constructivist teaching in the context of a chemistry topic, in *The Content of Science: a constructivist approach to its teaching and learning* (1994) and (with J. Leach and P. Scott) Learning Science, in *ASE Science Teachers Handbook* (1993).

Roger Beard is Senior Lecturer in Primary Education for the School of Education at the University of Leeds. He taught in primary schools and in a college of higher education before taking up his present post. He has written widely on children's literacy and development and his published works include *Children's Writing in the Primary School* (1984), *Developing Reading 3–13* (1990) *Teaching Literacy:*

Balancing Perspectives (1993) and *Rhyme, Reading and Writing* (1995).

Eileen Bellett is Chair of Theology, Religious and Cultural Studies at the University College of Ripon and York St John and is the tutor responsible for the Religious Education component in the initial teacher training programme there. She is also head of the National Society Centre of Religious Education at York. She has written *For People and Planet: exploring the link between Religious Education and economic awareness* (1991) and (with Monica Philbrick) *A Different Kind of Enterprise* (1991).

Helen Constable is a Research Officer for the School of Education at the University of Leeds. Her research interests include Design and Technological Capability in primary school children, the role of Evaluation within Art and Design and the application of Information Technology within Art and Design. She is the author of The role of drawing in designing and making – a primary perspective, in *Primary DATA* (1994 vol. 3, no. 2).

David Dawson is Visiting Part-time Lecturer to the School of Education at the University of Leeds and from 1982–92 was Senior Lecturer in Music Education at Bradford and Ilkley Community College. He was also editor and contributor for *Songs for Living* (1992) and *Hymns for Living* (1985). He made a major contribution to *Music for Everyone* (1985) and has written 'Three years in' – composition in class, for *Music Teacher* (1992). He has had various compositions published including *Four Blake Songs* (1991), *Hi-ee – Indian Chants* (1992) and *Four Canons for Christmas* (1993).

Carolyn Jones works at the centre for Physical Education/Sport at the University of Newcastle. She is the author of a number of articles on Physical Education in the Early Years and joint author or editor of a number of pedagogical texts on Physical Education (for children from 3–11 year olds) published by the University of Newcastle upon Tyne. A new text on Physical Education at Key Stage One is nearing completion. Her research interests are the processes of teaching and learning, through the medium of the physical, of children from pre-school to Key Stages One and Two. She is also currently Chair of the Physical Education Association Curriculum Committee and Vice President of the Association.

Ann MacNamara is Lecturer (Mathematics) for the School of Education at the University of Leeds. She works with Initial Teacher Training students and teachers on in-service and MEd courses. She has taught nursery, infant and junior children and contributed articles to professional journals in Mathematics Education and Curriculum and Assessment.

Patrick Wiegand is Senior Lecturer in Education (Geography) at the University of Leeds. His published works include *Children and Primary Geography* (1993) and *Places in the Primary School* (1992). He has edited five school atlases and associated classroom materials, co-edited the *New Oxford Children's Encyclopaedia* (1990) and has research interests in educational cartography and children's understanding of distant places.

Elizabeth Wood is a Lecturer for the School of Education at the University of Exeter. She specializes in the Early Years and Humanities. Her research interests include play, the development of children's understanding in history, and provision for the under-fives. She is author of several articles and two books *Educating the Under-fives* (1994) and *Play, Learning and the Early Years Curriculum* (1996).

PREFACE

'Who are YOU?' said the Caterpillar.
This was not an encouraging opening for a conversation. Alice
replied, rather shyly, 'I – I hardly know, Sir, just at present – at
least I know who I *was* when I got up this morning, but I think I
must have changed several times since then'.
                              Lewis Carroll, *Alice in Wonderland*

Alice's confused state of mind reflects that of primary teachers who
have struggled day by day to deal with the interminable changes in
educational reforms since 1988.

This book was written as a sequel to *The First Years at School*,
published at the start of the era of curriculum and assessment reform
in England and Wales. It provides an opportunity for a group of
colleagues, each an expert in their subject, but all united in a concern
for the education of young children, to try to make sense of the
changes. Though the author of each chapter speaks with a personal
voice, we worked collaboratively on the design and editing of the
book.

We pay tribute to the tenacity and resourcefulness of Key Stage
One teachers who, like Alice, managed to find a way through the
Wonderland.

GLOSSARY

Assessment of Performance Unit (APU)   A centrally funded unit set up to design and trial assessment instruments on a national sample of children; disbanded when SEAC was set up.

Attainment Targets (ATs)   Definable aspects of knowledge or skills specified for most subjects in the original National Curriculum Orders at ten levels.

Department for Education (DFE)   Previously Department for Education and Science (DES), with responsibility for science removed in 1992.

End of Key Stage Statements (EOKSS)   For Music, Art and Physical Education End of Key Stage Statements were defined in the Revised Orders for September 1995 to describe the types and ranges of performance which most pupils should characteristically demonstrate by the end of a key stage.

Grants for Education Support and Training (GEST)   Funding ear-marked by central government for training related to nationally identified in-service priorities.

Her Majesty's Inspectorate (HMI)   Formerly under the aegis of the Department for Education and Science but reorganized and made 'independent' as Office for Standards in Education (OFSTED).

INSET   In-service courses for the professional training and development of serving teachers.

Key Stages   The National Curriculum programmes of study were defined for four age ranges – 5 to 7-year-olds, 7 to 11-year-olds, 11 to 14-year-olds and 14 to 16-year-olds – each age phase described as a key stage.

Local Education Authorities (LEAs) Local Government committees in England and Wales with responsibility for educational institutions and services. Their powers were reduced by central government Acts of Parliament such as the 1988 Education Reform Act and the 1993 Education Act.

Local Education Authority Training Grants Scheme (LEATGS) Government funding for in-service courses for national priorities, devolved to Local Authorities, but with ring-fenced spending requirements.

Level Descriptors In the revised 1995 Orders these replaced Statements of Attainments. Teachers were expected to use their professional judgement as to which description 'best fits' a pupil's performance as a basis for a summary judgement.

Local Management of Schools (LMS) Devolvement of budgets for staffing, maintenance and services from Local Authority to school governing bodies' control.

National Curriculum Council (NCC) Established by the 1988 Education Reform Act with responsibility for the curriculum in state but not independent schools.

National Foundation for Educational Research (NFER) An independent organization with a brief to carry out contract educational research in England and Wales. Scotland and Ireland have their own research organizations.

Non-Statutory Guidance (NSG) Supplementary information/ advice for teachers included in the National Curriculum subject order folders.

Primary Assessment Curriculum and Experience (PACE) A major case-study of educational change set up in 1989 to examine the effects of the 1988 Education Act on British infant and primary schools.

Programmes of Study (POS) The detailed statutory content of each subject of the National Curriculum which teachers were required by law to 'deliver'.

Reading Recovery A New Zealand literacy intervention scheme aimed at 6-year-olds with limited reading and writing skills.

School Curriculum and Assessment Authority (SCAA) Replaced the previously separate bodies, National Curriculum Council and Schools Examination and Assessment Council in 1993.

School Examination and Assessment Council (SEAC) Established by the 1988 Education Reform Act with responsibility for curriculum and its assessment in schools.

Special Education Needs Coordinator (SENCO) A named teacher designated within a school, under the terms of a Code of Practice set up under the 1993 Education Act, with responsibility for administering 'stages' by which children with special educational needs are identified and catered for.

Standard Assessment Tasks (SATs) Tasks designed for 7, 11 and 14-year-olds to elicit a particular type of response in a standardized manner and to rate this, using standard methods, so that pupils could be assigned a level related to Attainment Targets in subjects.

Statements of Attainment (SoAs) Specific objectives defined for each of the ten levels of attainment in the Statutory Orders for each of the core and foundation subjects of the original National Curriculum.

Teacher Assessments (TAs) The formal assessments of children's achievements in the National Curriculum carried out by their teachers alongside the requirements of Standard Assessment Tasks.

1 A NATIONAL CURRICULUM FOR KEY STAGE ONE
Angela Anning

THE NEED FOR EDUCATIONAL REFORM

On 29 July 1988 the Education Reform Act became law in England and Wales. Since then Key Stage One teachers have experienced six turbulent years. In September 1989 they were swept into the mainstream of educational reform by the introduction of the three core subjects, English, Mathematics and Science, to Year One classes. Six of the foundation subjects – Technology, History, Geography, Art, Music and Physical Education – were introduced in successive waves over the next three years. The teaching of Religious Education was sustained by locally agreed syllabi drawn up within government guidelines. The effects of the Statutory Assessment requirements, particularly in the core subjects, for which Standard Assessment Tasks (SATs) for seven-year-olds were piloted in 1991 and modified each year, buffeted their teachers in four successive summer terms.

The speed and intensity of change produced chaotic working conditions in primary schools. The accusation has been made that the National Curriculum was 'pragmatic' rather than 'principled'. None of the changes were piloted. Consultation with grassroots teachers was derisory, often in windows of weeks during summer holidays. Information from government-funded evaluations of the effects of the reforms was carefully controlled (see Graham 1993). Alterations to Statutory Orders were implemented whilst schools were struggling to make current orders work. By comparison, in

Spain there has been a five-year build up to trialing some aspects of curriculum reform in schools, and in Holland acrimonious discussions about educational reform are still in full flow after twenty years!

Curriculum and assessment were not the only foci of government legislation to affect the education of young children. Under the Local Management of Schools initiative, control of school funding and employment was devolved from Local Authorities' declining power bases and budgets to the governing bodies and senior management of state schools. Harassed headteachers were required to learn new skills of accountancy and personnel management and deal with masses of paperwork. Government agencies were encouraging schools to 'opt out' of Local Authority control altogether into central government funding as grant-maintained schools. Only a handful of primary schools have done so, but the requirement to raise the question of whether or not to consider opting out, and if so to ballot parents, contributed to a sense of uncertainty about the future. Local Authority officers, themselves under enormous pressure to operate within declining budgets, were unable to offer the level of support headteachers had come to value. Models of teacher appraisal were being piloted across the country, and finally legislation was introduced to ensure that primary schools were inspected every four years. Her Majesty's Inspectors were 'detached' from the Department for Education and given the task of training large numbers of inspectors.

What was the purpose of this uncontrollable chaos? The seeds of educational reform were sown in the 1970s and 1980s. It was clear to everyone – employers, parents, politicians, administrators and teachers – that it was time for a coherent, 'broad and balanced' curriculum entitlement for all children in our state schools. (Private education in the United Kingdom has always been exempt from legislation of this kind.) However, each group had different motives for reform. Employers wanted improvements in standards, particularly those that fitted children for the needs of industry, and value for money. Parents wanted their children to 'be happy' in school and 'to do well', particularly in the basics of literacy and numeracy (D. Bennett 1987; Hughes *et al.* 1994). Politicians, badly 'rattled' by the teachers' union disputes of the 1970s and the influence of the liberal progressive ideologies of 'the educational establishment', wanted to use the reforms to make the state school system accountable to governing bodies, local communities and increasingly to a central system of monitoring and control. They believed that standards in state education were declining. Media coverage in the popular press often exacerbated public anxiety. 'For too long our children have been at the mercy of trendy "experts", bolshie unions and local councils with a political axe to grind' (*The Sun* 29 July 1992).

An influential group of right-wing educationists published a series of papers in the 1970s and 1980s pointing the way forward for reform (Cox and Boyson 1977; Hillgate Group 1986, 1987). The tone of their arguments is illustrated in the following extract:

Merit, competition and self-esteem have been devalued or repudiated; the teaching of facts has given way to the inculcation of opinion; education has often been confronted with indoctrination; in many places there is a serious risk of disciplined study being entirely swamped by an amorphous tide of easy-going discussion and idle play'

(Hillgate Group 1986: 2)

The vocabulary of child-centred education, experiential learning and a developmental curriculum espoused by early childhood educators became a target for derision. The pronouncements of the dominant political power group – mostly men (Margaret Thatcher was an honorary male exception), mostly educated in private schools, mostly deeply uncertain about women – gave clear messages about their value systems. For example, 'play' for them is essentially trivial, unless of course it takes place on a rugby pitch or golf course. Michael Fallon, then a minister within the Department of Education and Science, criticized the use of project work and was reported in the educational press at the time to have stated 'At worst this kind of practice turns the primary school into playgroups where there is much happiness and painting, but very little learning.' Similarly Kenneth Clarke, one of the fleeting ministers for education during the crucial period of reforms, criticizing 'child-centred' education, was reported to have claimed 'At its weakest there is a lot of sticking together of eggboxes and playing in the sand.'

The government appointees as senior administrators of the reforms used a language unfamiliar to primary school teachers – quality assurance mechanisms, value for money, preparation for employment – and claimed a Christian (meaning Church of England or Catholic) morality. They talked of sending in 'commando-style units' to sort out failing inner city schools. It was a language designed to bully and intimidate. In stark contrast the value systems of early childhood education emphasized the value of play as a powerful vehicle for learning, the importance of the social and emotional needs of the child, the significance of physicality and first-hand experiences, the need to develop literacy and numeracy as tools for learning and the importance of fun and enjoyment in motivating young children to want to learn. The discourses could not have been more different.

Government policy was driven by the New Right (see Ball 1994) harking back to 'traditional forms of education', Back to Basics, a return to 'disciplined' behaviour and competence in subjects. John Major intoned his version of 'education' at the 1992 Conservative Women's Conference 'Knowledge. Discipline. Tables. Sums. Dates. Shakespeare. British history. Standard English. Spelling. Marks. Tests. Good manners.'

Beyond the rhetoric there *was* research evidence of problems in primary education. Evidence from HMI Reports (DES 1978, 1982, 1990a) and research projects (Galton and Simon 1980; Bennett *et al.* 1984; Mortimore *et al.* 1988; Tizard *et al.* 1988; Alexander 1992) indicated that there already was a heavy emphasis on the 'basics' of literacy and numeracy in primary classrooms; undemanding work in geography and history (usually subsumed into project or topic work); teaching of dubious quality in science, and an unsystematic approach to assessment and record keeping.

What did infant teachers think about a National Curriculum? In May 1988 Child Education funded a national conference at York University on the proposed reforms (reported in *Child Education* 1988). The notes from discussion groups make fascinating retrospective reading in 1994. Most of the teachers at the conference broadly welcomed a National Curriculum and related system of assessment, reflecting research evidence from other studies of teachers' attitudes (Pollard *et al.* 1994; Evans *et al.* 1994). When asked what changes they anticipated in their classroom practice, they projected:

- time allocated to Science and Technology as new 'basics' will rise dramatically
- topic work will have to be 'redefined' so that subject strands will be more clearly identified
- music, art and physical education will be more effectively taught
- local will take second place to national concerns and priorities

- developmental issues will take second place to subject knowledge
- 4-year-olds in mixed age classes will be treated like 5-year-olds
- there will be a knock-on effect of test results of 7-year-olds on admission policies
- standardized testing of children in normal classroom settings will be difficult
- the use to which test results may be put (e.g. league tables of schools) will not benefit children, parents or schools
- the identification of starting points of the achievements of 5-year-olds will prove necessary, and these may offer evidence of the effectiveness of various types of pre-school provision.

The projections of this national sample of infant class teachers as the reforms were about to be introduced were to prove uncannily accurate. It makes it all the more tragic that grassroots opinion was not canvassed before radical reforms were implemented so that some of the more obvious problems might have been avoided.

Fundamental to the success of any major programme of educational reform is that changes in curriculum, assessment and pedagogy are tackled simultaneously. Initially, two separate agencies were established by the 1988 Act – The National Curriculum Council (NCC) based in York to advise the Secretary of State on all aspects of the school curriculum and the School Examination and Assessment Council (SEAC) based in London to advise on and oversee assessment. In October 1993, when the folly of separating policy and procedures for curriculum and assessment was impossible to ignore any longer, the two agencies were replaced by the London-based School Curriculum and Assessment Authority (SCAA). The way in which the reforms have affected these three interrelated aspects of education at Key Stage One – curriculum, assessment and pedagogy – will be addressed in turn.

CURRICULUM

The intention of curriculum reform was to provide education for children from the ages of 5 to 16 which was 'balanced and broadly based' (Sub-clause 1(2) of the Education Reform Act). The model chosen was the traditional secondary school subjects curriculum, with Technology assuming a new significance. In policy documents sponsored by government over the last five years the enhanced role of subject knowledge is signalled as central to the reform process. The Programmes of Study for each core and foundation subject were designed to a format comprising ten levels of Statements of Attainment. Working parties, dominated by secondary school and Higher Education subject specialists, wrote each order independently. Representation from the primary, especially Key Stage One, sector was scandalously limited. Nevertheless, the orders did reflect what infant teachers perceived to be 'good primary practice'. In 1989 the Early Years Curriculum Group claimed that 'A number of ideas which permeate these documents assent and affirm the very principles on which the early years curriculum is founded' (Early Years Curriculum Group 1989: 21).

However, for Early Years teachers with a deep-rooted belief in a curriculum based on children's developmental needs and interests, the dominance of subject knowledge in the professional discourse about the reforms left them feeling alienated and undervalued. Geva Blenkin and Vic Kelly (1988, 1994) have argued cogently for a reappraisal of what is a 'developmentally appropriate' curriculum for early childhood education. Others (Aubrey 1994; Edwards and Knight 1994) have argued that young children have an entitlement in their early years of schooling to an introduction to the discourse and disciplines of subjects, described by Alexander *et al.* (DES 1992, 21: 64) as 'some of the most powerful tools for making sense of the world which human beings have ever devised'. The fact is that a democratically elected government has legislated for Key Stage One teachers to 'deliver' subject knowledge to 5 to 7-year-olds, and we simply have to find a way to do so.

Traditionally, primary teachers have used topic work as a tool for ameliorating their uneasiness about teaching subjects. Research evidence has shown that English and Mathematics (often through the tyranny of commercial schemes) and Physical Education and Music (through the timetabling of hall space and in Music through the deployment of a specialist teacher) have usually been taught as discrete subjects. Throughout the period of reform infant teachers have persisted in using topics or themes as the basis for their curriculum planning (Cox and Sanders 1994; Pollard *et al.* 1994). In the early stages of reform, because of their preoccupation with the statutory requirements of assessment, teachers tended to focus on Statements of Attainment rather than Programmes of Study for their reference point to the Orders. However, there *have* been significant changes in their practice. The choice of a topic is no longer the 'property' of individual class teachers. They have lost the freedom and spontaneity of curriculum planning they previously enjoyed. Broad themes, usually to last a half-term in rolling two-year cycles, are determined at whole-school planning meetings. The quality of planning overall in primary schools has improved (DFE 1992; Bennett *et al.* 1992). A great deal of attention is paid to avoiding overlap in curriculum content for children, but also to providing opportunities for areas of enquiry to be revisited at different levels of challenge as children progress through the school.

Grudgingly, there has been a recognition that if topic work is to survive, it had better improve. Alexander *et al.* (DES 1992) argued that when topic work focuses on a clearly defined and limited number of Attainment Targets it can make an important contribution to the development of pupil learning. In *Primary Matters* (OFSTED 1994) factors associated with successful topic work were identified as an agreed whole-school system of planning and monitoring with sharing of teacher subject expertise, a fit with the Programmes of Study (using a single subject or grouping of subjects emphasis), and reference to specific learning outcomes and objectives with assessment opportunities built into the planning of activities.

Whatever planning strategies Key Stage One teachers tried, as waves of the Orders, each designed as self-contained units, swept through their classrooms, it became clear that there was an irreconcilable gap between the time available and their 'collective weight' as the then director of the National Curriculum Council was forced to admit (Pascall 1993). Ironically, as the government continued to exhort teachers to go Back to Basics, Key Stage One teachers were spending proportionately less time on reading (Raban *et al.* 1993) and Science (Campbell and Neill 1994). It was clear that laudable intentions of aiming for curriculum breadth were being subverted by sheer overload. In 1994 the government ordered a review of the National Curriculum, the Dearing Review. We will return to its recommendations in the final chapter.

In the six years of curriculum reform, infant teachers had worked 50-hour weeks to try to manage what in the end was officially acknowledged to be unmanageable (NCC 1993; OFSTED 1993). Pollard *et al.* (1994) have documented the stress levels of teachers. One teacher explained: 'There's a pressure and a feeling that you're never doing enough. You look at the documents and you think, "How can I possibly fulfil all these demands? How can I fit all this in?" It's just overwhelming sometimes.' Another said: 'You feel you're just going through a wheel. You're desperately covering stuff because you must give an assessment for it, and you think, "This is not what it's all about. Learning is not about this and this is not what it should be like"' (Pollard *et al.* 1994: 85).

Campbell and Neill (1994) argue that the conscientiousness of Key Stage One teachers was exploited. In describing their struggle to do the best for the children, some teachers adopted an almost missionary, self-sacrificing zeal. The demands of the job ate into their personal lives. A teacher in the Pollard study said: 'I don't believe a nun has any more dedication to her duties than I do' (Pollard *et al.* 1994: 90). Nowhere was this dedication more exploited than in the statutory demands of assessment to which we now turn.

ASSESSMENT

The Task Group on Assessment and Planning, headed by Paul Black, argued for a radical model of assessment at ages 7, 11 and 14 that was to be central to curriculum evaluation and planning. The group drew heavily on innovative work done by the Assessment of Performance Unit. A key paragraph of the TGAT Report read:

> Promoting children's learning is the principal aim of the school. Assessment lies at the heart of this process. It can provide a framework in which educational objectives be set and pupils' progress charted and expressed. It can yield a basis for planning the next educational steps in response to children's needs. By facilitating dialogue between teachers, it can enhance professional skills and help the school as a whole to strengthen learning across the curriculum and throughout its age range.
>
> (DES 1988)

In 1988 most teachers were daunted by the prospect of assessing the National Curriculum but broadly in sympathy with the TGAT Report model. It looked a reasonable alternative to the narrow range of standardized reading and mathematics tests that many local authorities had required in the past at the end of the infant phase of schooling. Any misgivings teachers had were based on a legacy of anxiety about 'labelling' children at too early an age and thus generating self-fulfilling prophecies about their capabilities. Teachers of young children had always been suspicious of accepting judgements recorded by colleagues during a previous phase (for example pre-school) or even class, claiming the right of every child to 'make a fresh start'. In fact there was evidence that teachers' judgements about children were often swiftly made, highly subjective, based on perceptions of a child's life outside school, and *did* have an effect on pupils' performances (Sharp and Green 1975; King 1978; for a summary of research evidence see Pilling and Kellmer Pringle 1978). In the TGAT proposals Teacher Assessments (TAs) were to be the focus for assessing and recording children's progress. Banks of Standard Assessment Tasks (SATs) were to be designed for teachers to administer at the end of each Key Stage, against which they might moderate their own TA judgements and those of other teachers. At aged 7, SATs were to be in English, Mathematics and Science. Most 7-year-olds were expected to achieve Level Two in these subjects.

Of all the reforms it was the implementation of the new assessment demands that produced the most anxiety (Bennett *et al.* 1992), and eventually outright hostility, amongst teachers. The tensions were partly due to conflicting messages about the purposes of assessment and testing, and partly to the technical difficulties of trying to make a complex system work. Politicians' purposes were to offer parents a mechanism for making judgements about schools and weeding out poor teachers, part of the market-led economy approach to sorting out the state school system. 'Schools will have to work to stay in business, and the worse their results, the more likely they will be to go to the wall' (Hillgate Group 1986: 16). John MacGregor, then Secretary of State for Education, talked about assessment as having 'the potential to lever up standards' (DES 1990a). League tables of school results were to be made available to the public through local and national newspapers to help parents to make choices about the 'best' school for their children.

It was intended that assessment should be manageable by a class teacher operating within 'normal' classroom constraints, with 7-year-olds working in groups of four to six, except for the individualized reading task. However, teachers were not allowed to intervene in the children's learning behaviours, and children and teachers naturally found this 'odd'. In most schools extra staff were drafted into Year Two classrooms during the SATs period to occupy the rest of the class whilst the class teacher carried out the testing with a small group. The demands of SATs disrupted 'normal' classrooms for several weeks. There was a vast amount of form filling to be done outside school hours – teachers reported 17 hours per week on average of extra administration, mostly in their own time. Local authorities were required to operate a system of moderation across schools, mostly done by primary advisers, but with no supply cover available, opportunities for class teachers to moderate their judgements were very limited. Each year teachers reported high levels of stress during the assessment periods (Shorrocks *et al.* 1992; Campbell and Neill 1994; Pollard *et al.* 1994).

The technical problems of operating a criterion-referenced model of assessment, a new experience for most infant teachers, were predictable but distressing. The definition of mastery levels in the models was like trying to nail jelly to the wall. Performance verbs like 'use', 'select', 'demonstrate' and 'understand' slid about all over the place as teachers tried to assess the level a child had achieved. Some of the Statements of Attainment were very specific – 'know and use addition and subtraction facts up to ten' – and some were incredibly vague – 'participate in a presentation'. Some contained a huge range of elements – 'find books or magazines in a class or school library by using the classification system, catalogue or database and use appropriate methods of finding information, when pursuing a line of enquiry'. Mastery level judgements assigned children to different levels on the basis of apparently trivial criterion changes. For example, in the 1991 pilot SATs mastery Level 2 in Writing required a child to use 'at least two capital letters and at least two full stops' and for Level 3 'more than half, and at least five sentences correctly punctuated'. Only 38 per cent of the pilot sample children met Level 2 criteria and 18 per cent reached Level 3. A slight shift in the wording of each Attainment Target could radically alter these percentages. Such shifts were made year by year by the SAT designers working to School Examination and Assessment Council staff demands, which in turn were determined by government requirements. This meant that any talk of advances or declines in standards at age 7 were spurious claims. Inevitably, the lack of clarity in the criteria produced variations in teachers ascribing children to levels of attainment.

The crude system of aggregating children's scores on several Attainment Targets within profile components in each subject (for example, levels achieved in writing, spelling and handwriting in the profile component Writing in the English Order) and then aggregating profile component scores (for example, in English Speaking and Listening, Reading and Writing) for a subject level score meant that at each point of aggregation, the level of potentially useful diagnostic detail, was progressively blurred into global and unhelpful summative judgements. The mental baggage of norm referencing in testing clouded teachers' responses to level statements. They began to talk about 'a Level 2 sort of child', for those of average ability. Mary Jane Drummond argued passionately against this labelling:

> Assigning young children to one of three or four levels of achievement may have the undesirable outcome of creating a new category of underachievement: the 'Level One Child'. The purpose of compiling numerical data on every child's performance on each attainment target may be to achieve accuracy and objectivity (which may well prove to be illusory); but the outcome may be a rigid stratification of pupils based on a string of numbers they carry round with them in their record folders.
>
> (Drummond 1993)

The claim that SAT results were 'standardized' (SEAC 1991) was questioned by the findings of several research projects (Shorrocks *et al.* 1993; Campbell and Neill 1994; Pollard *et al.* 1994). Different classroom contexts, variations in extra adult support in the classroom, teachers' strategies to minimize pupils' anxieties about the tests, all affected children's ability to demonstrate what they could achieve.

Politically unpalatable data about the background variables from the ENCA project (Shorrocks *et al.*, 1992) evaluating the first round of assessment in 1992, were that as well as social background, the birthdate, first language and effects of nursery education all had significant effects on the SAT results of 7-year-olds. Summer-born children achieved significantly lower levels, bilingual children scored lower if English was their second language (unless, as in Wales, their first language was used to deliver the assessment tasks), and children who had attended nurseries (particularly in inner city areas) achieved higher levels in English and Mathematics, but not in Science tasks.

A 'backlash' effect of the new requirement for teacher assessments has been an explosion of record-keeping systems in primary schools. Teachers were advised to keep evidence to substantiate their Teacher Assessments, which they were required to present formally as part of an annual report on each child for parents. The government and media emphasis on teacher accountability persuaded teachers that they would be judged by their pupils' test results. They devised detailed, time-consuming, often tick-list based systems of record keeping (Evans *et al.* 1994), described by HMI as 'fervent but unfocused' (DES 1990b). With systems often duplicated for class, school and national reporting purposes, form filling exacerbated the erosion of teachers' time for personal and family lives. Campbell *et al.* (1994) reported that infant teachers were regularly working a 50-hour week. As teachers' anxieties were fuelled by media reports of falling standards and poor league table results, they began to demand baseline testing of all children at school entry, so that it would be clear to parents how much a school had moved on a cohort of children during their infant schooling. For a discussion of types of school entry assessment systems in use see Cline and Blatchford (1994).

In their excellent book, *Assessment in Early Childhood Education*, Blenkin and Kelly (1992: 20–1) argue that the SEAC assessment programme 'represents an emphasis on the use of assessment for summative and administrative purposes rather than for purposes which might be described as formative or educational. It can further be seen as an attempt to use assessment as a form of control'. If we return to the conflicts of values referred to in the first section of this chapter, we can see how the programme served the needs of politicians, administrators, parents and perhaps teachers, but it is hard to see how it served the needs of children. Essentially, an educationally sound assessment system should alert both learners and teachers to what children can do, so that they can move on to what they might do next – what Vygotsky called the buds rather than the fruits of development. Sadly, despite all the hard work teachers put into trying to make the model work, there is little evidence that the assessments fed directly back into the next planned sequence of curriculum activities as the TGAT model had proposed they should.

PEDAGOGY

This is the third and least understood area of primary education. What used to be 'the secret garden' of the school curriculum has been neatly divided into beds; assessment has been dug, raked and hoed but pedagogy remains a wilderness.

When the reforms were initiated, the documentation from DES emphasized that pedagogy was the property of schools. 'The National Curriculum . . . provides for greater clarity and precision about what should be taught while enabling schools to retain flexibility about how they organise teaching' (NCC 1989). By 1992, the so-called Three Wise Men (Alexander, Woodhead and Rose) were commissioned to review research evidence about 'the delivery' of education in primary schools and 'make recommendations about curriculum organisation, teaching methods and classroom practice appropriate for the successful implementation of the National Curriculum, particularly at Key Stage 2.' Much of what was argued about pedagogy in the document was decontextualized and used for their own purposes by politicians, sensationalized by some press coverage and inappropriately generalized to the education of children at Key Stage One. The tone of some of the decontextualized sentences sounded ominous to infant teachers – 'Over the last few decades the progress of primary pupils has been hampered by the influence of highly questionable dogmas which have led to excessively complex classroom practices' (DES 1992: 3.2); 'we believe there are many circumstances in which it is more appropriate to tell than to ask' (ibid: 104). Such assertions antagonized lobbyists for a child-centred curriculum.

A review of research evidence relevant to the education of young children was drawn up by David, Curtis and Siraj-Blatchford – 'we felt it imperative to write an early years "report", a short, complementary "sister guide"' (David *et al.* 1993). The report pointed to research evidence about the significance of practical, experiential learning; the social context of learning; the vital role of adult intervention in 'scaffolding' children's learning; the ineffectiveness of lengthy periods of whole-class teaching for young children; and the dangers of introducing them to a too formal curriculum too soon. Their report received little of the razzmatazz of media attention given to the Three Wise Men report.

Since 1992 a series of central government discussion documents has been published with a new emphasis on pedagogy. They are littered with references to the importance of 'subject knowledge' and 'expository teaching' for improving practice in primary classrooms. For example, in a follow-up to the 1992 report, it was argued that 'the amount and quality of expository teaching received by pupils, including giving clear explanations, asking relevant questions and responding effectively to their questions and answers, was often too slight' (OFSTED 1993: 8.8); 'there were more satisfactory or good lessons where the number of different activities undertaken at any one time was limited, usually to a manageable number of four or less' (ibid; 9.9) and 'although teachers frequently exploited the potential of whole-class teaching for younger pupils in the case of literature, there was much less evidence of their doing so in subjects where it might have brought similar benefits, such as history, geography and science' (ibid: 9.12).

In 1994, *Primary Matters*, a review drawing on OFSTED evidence of the impact of the National Curriculum on primary classroom organization and practice, listed the most significant factors associated with high standards of achievement in this order: satisfactory or good knowledge of the subject; good questioning skills; effective use of exposition, instruction and direct teaching; good balance of grouping strategies; effective use of ability teaching – whole class, small group or individual as appropriate (OFSTED 1994). Such coded messages from DFE-speak are deeply worrying to Key Stage One teachers. Many are successfully organizing young children's learning around small group teaching, practical workshop or structured play-based activities, with a strong emphasis on literacy and numeracy and a broader curriculum based on what interests and motivates young learners. As a predominantly female workforce, they feel that their valuable and valid professional experience and discourse, based on working on a daily basis both with young children and their carers, is being eroded by men in grey suits with little understanding of early childhood education.

The Key Stage One teachers observed in the PACE project 'in response to the pressures of the National Curriculum and assessment, appeared to be adapting by tightening their classroom control and by providing more direction to children's activities' (Pollard *et al.* 1994: 166). Yet the overall balance between whole class, group and individualized teaching commended by the Three Wise Men was 'already being practised by half the teachers'. In Campbell's study, teachers were questioned about their classroom practice, but not observed. They claimed substantial improvements in planning with colleagues and assessing pupils' learning, but little change in teaching methods (Campbell and Neill 1994: 92). Areas where they felt standards had fallen were in catering for children with special educational needs, an issue to which we will return in the final chapter, and in the teaching of reading. They claimed that both those crucial aspects of the education of young children were being squeezed out by the excessive demands of curriculum and assessment reform.

The reforms were premised on the core and foundation subjects being 'delivered' to all Key Stage One children. In the following chapters each author will examine aspects of change in the education of young children in their 'own' subject discipline.

REFERENCES

Alexander, R.J. (1992) *Policy and Practice in Primary Education*. London: Routledge.
Aubrey, C. (ed.) (1994) *The Role of Subject Knowledge in the Early Years of Schooling*. London: Falmer Press.
Ball, S.J. (1994) *Education Reform: A Critical and Post-structural Approach*. Buckingham: Open University Press.
Bennett, D. (1987) The aims of teachers and parents for children in their first year at school, in S. Cleave and S. Brown (eds) *Four Year Olds in School: Policy and Practice,* NFER/SCDC Report. Windsor: NFER.
Bennett, S.N., Desforges, C., Cockburn, A. and Wilkinson, B. (1984) *The Quality of Pupil Learning Experiences*. London: Lawrence Erlbaum Associates.
Bennett, S.N., Wragg, E.C., Carré, C.G. and Carter, D.G. (1992) A longitudinal study of primary teachers' perceived competence in and concerns about National Curriculum implementation. *Research Papers in Education,* 7: 53–78.
Blenkin, G.V. and Kelly, A.V. (eds) (1988) *Early Childhood Education: A Developmental Curriculum*. London: Paul Chapman Publishing Ltd.
Blenkin, G.V. and Kelly, A.V. (1992) *Assessment in Early Childhood Education*. London: Paul Chapman Publishing Ltd.
Blenkin, G.V. and Kelly, A.V. (eds) (1994) *A National Curriculum and Early Learning: An Evaluation*. London: Paul Chapman Publishing Ltd.
Campbell, R.J. and Neill, S.R. St.J. (1994) *Curriculum Reform at Key Stage One: Teacher Commitment and Policy Failure*. Harlow: Longman/Association of Teachers and Lecturers.
Child Education (1988) Editorial. September, 65(9): 8–9.
Cline, T. and Blatchford, P. (1994) Baseline assessment: selecting a method of assessing children of school entry, *Education 3–13,* 22(3): 10–15.
Cox, C.B. and Boyson, R. (eds) (1977) *Black Paper 1977*. London: Temple Smith.
Cox, T. and Sanders, S. (1994) *The Impact of the National Curriculum on the Teaching of Five Year Olds*. London: Falmer Press.
David, T., Curtis, A. and Siraj-Blatchford, I. (1993) *Effective Teaching in the Early Years: Fostering Children's Learning in Nurseries and in Infant Classes,* an OMEP (UK) Report. University of Warwick: OMEP (Organisation Mondiale pour l'Education Préscolaire).

DES (1978) *Primary Education in England: A Survey by Her Majesty's Inspectors.* London: HMSO.

DES (1982) *Education 5–9, An Illustrative Survey.* London: HMSO.

DES (1988) *National Curriculum. Task Group on Assessment and Testing. A Report.* London: HMSO.

DES (1990a) *Speeches on Education: National Curriculum and Assessment.* London: HMSO.

DES (1990b) *Standards in Education 1988–89. The Annual Report of Her Majesty's Chief Inspector of Schools.* London: HMSO.

DES (1992) *Curriculum Organisation and Classroom Practice in Primary Schools: A Discussion Paper.* London: HMSO.

DFE (1992) *Education Observed. The Implementation of the Curriculum Requirements of ERA: An Overview by HM Inspectorate on the Second Year.* London: HMSO.

Drummond, M.J. (1993) *Assessing Children's Learning.* London: David Fulton.

Early Years Curriculum Group (1989) *The Early Years and the National Curriculum.* Stoke-on-Trent: Trentham Books Ltd.

Edwards, A. and Knight, P. (1994) *Effective Early Years Education.* Buckingham: Open University Press.

Evans, L., Packwood, A., Neill, S.R. St.J. and Campbell, J. (1994) *The Meaning of Infant Teachers' Work.* London: Routledge.

Galton, M. and Simon, B. (1980) *Inside the Primary Classroom.* London: Routledge and Kegan Paul.

Graham, D. (1993) *A Lesson for Us All: The Making of the National Curriculum.* London: Routledge.

Hillgate Group (1986) *Whose Schools? A Radical Manifesto.* London: Claridge Press.

Hillgate Group (1987) *Reform of British Education.* London: Claridge Press.

Hughes, M., Wikeley, F. and Nash, T. (1994) *Parents and their Children's Schools.* Oxford: Blackwell.

King, R. (1978) *All Things Bright and Beautiful? A Sociological Study of Infants Classrooms.* Bath: John Wiley.

Mortimore, P., Sammons, P., Stoll, L., Lewis, D. and Eob, R. (1988) *School Matters. The Junior Years.* London: Open Books.

NCC (1989) *Curriculum Guidance: A Framework for the Primary Curriculum.* York: National Curriculum Council.

NCC (1993) *The National Curriculum at Key Stages 1 and 2; Advice to the Secretary of State for Education.* York: National Curriculum Council.

OFSTED (Office for Standards in Education) (1993) *Curriculum Organisation and Classroom Practice in Primary Schools. A Follow-up Report.* London: DFE Publications Centre.

OFSTED (1994) *Primary Matters. A Discussion on Teaching and Learning in Primary Schools.* London: OFSTED Publications Centre.

Pascall, D., (1993) *In Pursuit of Excellence,* Conference of Cambridgeshire Primary Heads: University of Leicester.

Pilling, D. and Kellmer Pringle, M. (1978) *Controversial Issues in Child Development.* London: Paul Elek for National Children's Bureau.

Pollard, A., Broadfoot, P., Croll, P., Osborn, M., Abbot, D. (1994) *Changing English Primary Schools? The Impact of the Education Reform Act at Key Stage One.* London: Cassell.

Raban, B., Clark, U. and MacIntyre, J. (1993) *Evaluation of the Implementation of English in the National Curriculum at Key Stages 1, 2 and 3 (1991–93).* York: National Curriculum Council/University of Warwick.

SEAC (1991) *A Handbook of Guidance for the SATs.* London: HMSO.

Sharp, R. and Green, A. (1975) *Education and Social Control. A Study in Progressive Primary Education.* London: Routledge and Kegan Paul.

Shorrocks, D., Daniels, S., Stainton, R., Ring, K. (1992) *Testing and Assessing 6 and 7 Year Olds; The Evaluation of the 1992 Key Stage 1 National Curriculum Assessment. Final Report.* National Union of Teachers and School of Education, University of Leeds. London: National Union of Teachers.

Shorrocks, D., Frobisher, L., Nelson, N., Turner, L. and Waterson, A. (1993) *Implementing National Curriculum Assessment in the Primary School.* London: Hodder and Stoughton.

Tizard, B., Blatchford, P., Bourke, J., Farquar, C. and Plewis, I. (1988) *Young Children at School in the Inner City.* London: Lawrence Erlbaum.

2 ENGLISH

Roger Beard

THE NATIONAL CURRICULUM REWRITE

It is not always appreciated how much the decision to rewrite the
National Curriculum Order for English was related to evaluation
studies involving hundreds of Key Stage One teachers. This chapter
will summarize the main findings from these studies and also show
how parts of the English Order were not as helpful in supporting
classroom practices as they might have been. It will be suggested that
some aspects of the National Curriculum in English may have been
disproportionately influenced by the radical ideas of the 1980s
which had not yet been subjected to detailed critical analysis. The
chapter will end by looking to the future. It will draw on the
implications of recent research and publications for Early Years
English teaching in the five years after 1995, when the National
Curriculum is to remain unchanged.

THE EVALUATION OF NATIONAL CURRICULUM
ENGLISH 1989–93

Maintained schools were obliged to implement the National Curriculum Order from the autumn of 1989. Almost immediately
evaluations began of the implementation. A few months later, the
National Curriculum Council (NCC) was able to identify several

'key issues' which required further investigation to see if the Curriculum needed some rewriting. These issues were identified from a survey administered by the National Foundation for Educational Research (NFER), which sent 2,300 questionnaires to schools, and from case study visits to 33 schools in eight LEAs. For Key Stage One teachers, questionnaires were directed to those who taught Year 1.

The findings from the above were considered by the National Curriculum Council alongside reports from Her Majesty's Inspectors, based on HMI's visits to 350 classes containing Year 1 children during 1989–90 and further visits by HMI to 360 classes of other Early Years age ranges (NCC 1991). The University of Warwick was commissioned to investigate the following 'key issues' in relation to the teaching of English in Key Stage One.

In Reading:

- whether the gap between Levels 1 and 2 was too wide
- whether the Non-Statutory Guidance (NSG) encouraged the necessary mix of teaching methods and, in particular, placed appropriate emphasis on the teaching of phonics
- whether the NSG offered sufficiently clear advice on classroom management skills for meeting the needs of individual children.

In Writing:

- whether the statements of attainment for Level 1 were pitched at the wrong level
- whether the gap between Levels 1 and 2 was too wide.

In Speaking and Listening:

- whether teachers were able to give appropriate time to this attainment target and, if not, what the reasons were.

In Knowledge about Language:

- whether statements on knowledge about language needed reorganization or reformulation and what these should be
- which parts of Knowledge about Language would enhance the learning of language and grammar at Levels 1–4

• whether additional Statements of Attainment should be formu-
lated.

These issues are largely derived from what teachers had reported
in the 1989–90 NCC evaluation (NCC 1991). Case study findings
had confirmed that the 'leaps' between Levels 1 and 2 in Reading and
Writing were a particular problem. It is worth providing a reminder
of the size of these leaps by setting out some representative criteria
from each aspect.

> From Reading, Level 1: 'begin to recognise individual words or
> letters in familiar contexts';
>
> From Reading, Level 2: 'read a range of material with some
> independence, fluency, accuracy and understanding' (DES
> 1989: 7).
>
> From Writing, Level 1: 'use pictures, symbols, or isolated
> letters, words or phrases to communicate meaning';
>
> From Writing, Level 2: 'produce, independently, pieces of
> writing using complete sentences, some of them demarcated
> with capital letters and full stops or question marks'
> (DES 1989: 12)

Historians of Education may look back at these parts of the first
National Curriculum with some surprise, given the lack of detailed
support in the Programmes of Study and Non-Statutory Guidance
(NSG). In relation to Reading, for instance, there is hardly any
reference to the phonological aspects of Reading, even though
written English is an alphabetic system, in which letters represent
speech sounds. The phonics teaching approach receives just one
specific mention in the whole of the Order and then in a phrase which
appears to give it a similar status to 'picture cues' (DES 1989: 7). The
NSG only specifies a 'shared' or 'apprenticeship' approach and, in a
rather derelict way, suggests that 'Teachers will decide how much
support the child will need' (DES 1989: B5). It is not surprising to
read in the NCC evaluation report that 'the omission of the "wealth
of work" to be undertaken between the levels was pointed out many
times' (NCC 1991: 50).

Concerns regarding 'knowledge about language' appear not to
have figured centrally in the findings from the 1989–90 evaluation,
perhaps because this aspect was not directly referred to either in the

Attainment Targets or in the Programmes of Study for Early Years teachers.

THE WARWICK STUDY

The Warwick evaluation, which focused on the above issues and some others more related to Key Stages Two and Three, began in the autumn of 1991 and was scheduled to run for two years. The general brief of the evaluation was to gauge whether any problems in implementing the Order were the result of the Order itself, whether it was a question of teacher knowledge and understanding, or whether Statements of Attainment were pitched inappropriately for pupils in particular Key Stages (Raban *et al.* 1994).

After a detailed initial analysis of the Order, 2,000 questionnaires (of which about 30 per cent were returned) were sent out to a sample of schools selected to be representative of a range of school size, type and catchment in all three Key Stages. The project staff also spent 15 months visiting schools, talking to teachers and observing in classrooms. In all 60 schools were visited in seven LEAs not covered in the postal survey. Interviews were undertaken with headteachers, English coordinators and class teachers, who also returned diaries which they kept of their work. School policies were inspected and discussions were held with whole-school teaching staffs.

Detailed classroom observations were made through 269 sessions, across three Key Stages. The Warwick study provides extensive evidence of how Key Stage One teachers were translating the subject orders, and the related assessment requirements, into workable curricula and strategies for the monitoring of children's learning in their classrooms. As well as investigating the 'key issues' outlined earlier in this chapter, the project also included a study of the general manageability of the English Order.

General manageability

The study addressed the relationship between English as a subject and English as used in different topics. The study found that teachers were using Schemes of Work predominantly to ensure coverage of the National Curriculum requirements and less to plan for differentiation, progression and the monitoring of individual achievement. Key Stage One teachers in all schools thought that there was

Table 1   Observed time (in minutes) spent on English as a separate subject and English within other subjects

| Attainment Targets | Key Stage One | | | |
| | English | | X-curricular English | |
	Minutes	%	Minutes	%
AT1 Speaking and Listening	550	17	599	18
AT2 Reading	1208	37	68	2
AT3–5 Writing (inc. spelling and handwriting)	648	20	179	6
Totals	2406	74	846	26
Total time observed	3278 mins 100%			

insufficient time to teach the full curriculum satisfactorily and especially to hear reading. They were concerned about the pressures and demands of other foundation subject orders and felt that these should be reduced.

There was an interesting discrepancy between the survey findings and the classroom observations: 72 per cent of Key Stage One teachers said that their main way of teaching English was through cross-curricular topic work rather than through English as a separate subject. However, the observations suggested that the reverse was true in Reading and Writing, as Table 1 shows, and in Speaking and Listening the observed times are about the same.

Table 2   Percentage of responses indicating areas of change in teaching English

| | Key Stage One | |
	English coordinator %	Class teacher %
Content	28	27
Teaching methods	19	22
Time allocations	19	18
Administration	34	33
Totals	100	100

When Key Stage One teachers were asked about changes in the way they taught English, administration was seen to be the major area of change since the National Curriculum had been introduced, as can be seen in Table 2.

The main changes in the content of what was taught were felt to be an increased emphasis on Spelling, Handwriting and Grammar. In three of the case study schools, cursive writing was being introduced in the Reception class as a direct result of the Key Stage One Standard Assessment Tasks (SATs), to help some children to achieve Level 3 of the Writing Attainment Target, which demanded it. In teaching methods, the changes were felt to be towards greater formality; in time allocation, teachers perceived that there was simply insufficient time to allocate. These findings from the survey were confirmed in the interviews and case studies.

Reading

Was the gap between Levels 1 and 2 too wide?
The researchers found that teachers monitored pupils' progress between Levels 1 and 2 by keeping records and by recording book titles, rather than by tracking pupils' progress with the help of a 'conceptual map' of reading development. As Table 3 shows, however, there was a general emphasis on building up a sight vocabulary which gradually shifted to a greater emphasis on the use of phonic cues. In general it seems that the 'gap problem' between Levels 1 and 2 of the National Curriculum in Reading could have been avoided if the framework had been more closely built on established practices of teachers.

In the interviews, the majority of teachers expressed dissatisfaction with the gap, particularly because of the problems it raised for assessment. Level 1 was felt to be too easily achieved, while Level 2 was too broad and difficult. There were problems explaining to parents why some pupils remained working at Level 2 for such a long time. The problems were compounded by teachers' uncertainties in interpreting the word 'some' in Statement of Attainment (SoA) 2f, which was referred to earlier: 'read a range of material with some independence, fluency, accuracy and understanding'. This uncertainty was possibly linked to the fact that fewer children achieved this SoA than the other five SoAs.

Table 3   Percentage of Reading activities commonly identified in the National Survey

	Reception %	Year 1 %	Year 2 %
Developing recognition of individual words by sight	24*	14	12
Practising sounding individual letters	21*	14	7
Developing knowledge and use of the alphabet	15	15	15
Using phonic cues for new words	18	23*	22*
Reading new words informed by use of context	17	18	22*
Practising sounding groups of letters	5	16	22*
Totals	100	100	100

*   Most frequently mentioned.

The necessary mix of methods

In relation to the key issue of the 'necessary mix' of teaching methods, Key Stage One teachers reported in interviews that they were now spending less time on hearing children read. As an Early Years teacher reported in another study 'The actual hearing children read and doing the background work to reading so that they're [the children] being read to, that sort of thing is being missed out' (Nina, cited in Evans *et al.* 1994: 115).

This reduction in the frequency of hearing children read was apparently due partly to the demands of other subjects and partly to teachers needing to broaden their approach in order to meet the National Curriculum requirements that children should talk about what they had read.

Of the methods of teaching Reading observed by the researchers, by far the most commonly used approach was to have a pupil reading from a book (including talking about the reading) with a teacher or another adult, which took up half the total observed time. The second most observed teaching approach was phonics (16 per cent of observed time), followed by pupils reading to themselves or listening to reading (9 per cent each), whole word recognition (8 per cent) and repetition and practice activities (7 per cent). In terms of observed time spent by children themselves on reading activities, however, the balance was rather different, with phonics activities taking up over 24 per cent of time, followed by reading to a teacher or other adult (23 per cent). The other kinds of reading activities listed above each took up about an eighth of observed pupil time.

There are clear signs, then, that there was a mismatch between the National Curriculum and teachers' practices, especially in connection with the teaching of phonics. It is important to note, though, that 68 per cent of the observed phonics activities occurred as 'self-contained' exercises and there is a tension here with the implications of recent research, as will be discussed at the end of this chapter.

Did the NSG provide appropriate advice on classroom management skills?

About a third of teachers had found the NSG useful, a third had not and a third felt that they needed more time to digest it. The analysis of the Order by the project team suggested that, while there were ideas on classroom management, these were targeted mainly at Speaking and Listening. The subsequent classroom observations indicated that, at Key Stage One, half of teachers' management time was occupied with resources, whilst classroom organization and people management (colleagues, parents, helpers, etc.) took about a quarter each.

Writing

Were the Statements of Attainment for Level 1 pitched at the wrong level? Was the gap between Levels 1 and 2 too wide?

The investigations of these two questions seem to be best discussed together. Three-quarters of teachers interviewed were dissatisfied with the progression between Levels 1 and 2. They felt that Level 1 was achievable with some ease, whereas Level 2 seemed rather demanding and there was an additional problem with the wording of SoA 2a: 'produce independently, pieces of writing using complete sentences, some of them demarcated with capital letters and full stops or question marks' (DES 1989: 12). What was 'some' supposed to mean? LEA guidance on this understandably varied from one Authority to another. Perhaps as a consequence, in the first two years of the SATs assessments SoA 2a was achieved by fewer pupils than the other three SoAs at Level 2 in Writing.

Table 4   Percentage of teaching Writing activities observed in Key Stage One classrooms

Activities	%
Composing	
Teacher scribing for pupil exactly what s/he says	11
Teacher scribing for pupil re-phrasing what s/he says	3
Collaborative writing	6
Pupils draw pictures and 'scribble-write' underneath	4
Breakthrough to literacy materials	3
Computer used by pupils to compose their writing	3
Teacher provides opportunities for pupils to write independently	39
Teacher writes to pupil dictation to provide a model for copying	4
Total	73
Secretarial	
Teacher writes in pupil's book for pupil to copy	4
Teacher writes on the board for pupil to copy	7
Teacher uses phonics in a sound/symbol approach to spelling	4
Workbooks/dictionaries/print environment used to aid and support writing	12
Total	27

Table 4 shows the range and distribution of activities which were observed in Key Stage One classrooms in both the composing of writing and 'presentational' aspects.

It is interesting to note that, in the interviews, teachers said they were now placing more emphasis on promoting independent writing in order to prepare their pupils for the SAT, but that they had misgivings about this. Teachers were worried that the requirement to write independently *and* punctuate correctly at such an early age had led to many pupils formulating shorter pieces of writing, comprising single clause sentences, than they might have produced in pre-SAT days. Teachers identified the main changes in their teaching since the introduction of the National Curriculum as using a wider range of forms of writing, more emphasis on 'emergent writing', and a greater emphasis on drafting and editing, grammar and punctuation. These changes generally corresponded with other sources of data in the evaluation, although the researchers rarely observed as much variation of writing in different forms as was reported to them and rarely did they see the drafting and editing which had been referred to in survey returns.

In spelling and handwriting there was also evidence of teaching being more influenced by the assessment requirements than by the Order itself. They reported teaching cursive writing at an earlier stage and teaching spelling more formally and more to groups and to the whole class than before. However, the observations did not always confirm this: the most commonly observed teaching of handwriting and spelling was on an individual basis. In fact, across all three Key Stages there seemed to be very little explicit teaching of 'regular' and 'irregular' spelling patterns.

Speaking and Listening

*Were teachers able to give appropriate time to this
Attainment Target?*
Despite teachers' fears, the classroom observations indicated that their attention was not skewed away from this Attainment Target. In Key Stage One, it took nearly 18 per cent of 'sole focus' time, most of this time being more related to Reading than to any other Attainment Target. A big majority of Key Stage One teachers welcomed the provision of this Attainment Target and felt that their teaching had changed through an increased awareness of the importance of providing more opportunities for Speaking and Listening.

Knowledge about Language

*Did the Statements of Attainment need reorganization or
reformulation? What Statements of Attainment should these
be and which parts of knowledge about language would
enhance the learning of language and grammar?*
The researchers found that teachers were uncertain as to the definition and scope of 'knowledge about language'. The English Order was found to be unhelpful in this respect. Teachers in Key Stage One were fully aware of the requirements for teaching grammar and punctuation. There was agreement that explicit references to the teaching of knowledge about language could and should be extended to below Level 5.

CHANGES FOLLOWING THE WARWICK STUDY

The Warwick evaluation therefore provided a multilayered and finely grained investigation into the implementation of the English

National Curriculum. A year into the project, the National Curriculum Council advised the Secretary of State that the English Order did need to be revised (NCC 1992). This decision was apparently influenced by the first interim report which the Warwick research provided, as well as by other sources including two separate NFER reports – one on reading standards *Reading in Recession* (Gorman and Fernandes 1992) and one on the teaching of early literacy (Cato *et al.* 1992) – also reports from HMI, the DES and professional associations.

In its advice to the Secretary of State, the NCC summed up the achievements of the English Order but also recommended where the revision should provide a clearer framework for Early Years teachers for future years.

In Speaking and Listening:

- there should be more emphasis on pupils becoming confident users of standard English
- there should be greater emphasis on listening skills.

In Reading:

- there should be more detailed reference to the skills which need to be taught if children are to learn to read
- the gap between Levels 1 and 2 should be smaller
- the Order should be more balanced in the emphasis which it gives to methods of teaching children to read, including the use of reading schemes (which were not mentioned at all in the Order) and phonics (which was only briefly mentioned once).

In Writing:

- there should be a clearer definition of basic skills
- the criteria for attaining Level 1 should be raised, thus representing real 'achievement'
- spelling and handwriting should be integrated within the Writing Attainment Target.

In Knowledge about Language:

- references to Knowledge about Language in the English Order should begin earlier than Level 5

- grammatical understanding should be defined with greater precision
- a greater range of activities should be referred to which can help develop spelling ability.

These proposals became part of the Dearing Review which condensed the National Curriculum.

LEARNING FROM LOOKING BACK

Looking back on the National Curriculum in English, it is illuminating to ask why there were several central weaknesses which were identified in its very first year. These were self-evidently going to pose big challenges, especially the wide gaps between Levels 1 and 2 in Reading and Writing and the lack of convincing guidance to help bridge these gaps.

One explanation may be that the National Curriculum was planned to try to accommodate different ideologies. The original Level 2 details in Reading and Writing reflected more traditional notions of attainment; Level 1 reflected a more 'emergent' perspective. Publications about the former had not generally made concessions to the notion of 'emergent literacy', a term originally coined by Marie Clay (1966) to refer to 'partly formed' early literacy; publications about the latter had not always accounted for the way that approximations in reading and writing are developed into increasingly skilled performance. The one member of the English Working Party who knew the Key Stage One English area well, Professor Katharine Perera, was invited to join the Committee after the Key Stage One recommendations had been completed and then only as a replacement for the author Roald Dahl (Bald 1993: 25).

Similarly, the lack of reference to reading schemes and phonological processes in reading and the apparent over-reliance on the apprenticeship approach in the NSG may have been symptomatic of the *Zeitgeist* of the late 1980s in both initial teacher training and in-service provision. The National Curriculum Working Party could have been caught up in something akin to the Emperor's New Clothes in relation to the validity of some of these ideas. Subsequent research and critical analyses exposed how problematic several of the ideas were. Marilyn Jager Adams (1990), in a report commissioned by the USA Congress, provided strong evidence of the importance of systematic phonics teaching. Katharine Perera (1993) compared a selection of reading schemes and 'real' or individual books and showed how misleading it can be to draw polarized distinctions between them. This study also provides many insights and principles for schools to use when choosing a new reading scheme or approach. The critique of the apprenticeship approach by Jane Oakhill and myself (Beard and Oakhill 1994) suggests that it may have been rather premature for the NSG to give this approach the status which it did.

LEARNING FROM LOOKING FORWARD

For the immediate future, the concerns of all Early Years teachers must be to study and to explore with their colleagues how best to use the 20 per cent of time which is intended under the terms of the Dearing Review to be released from direct National Curriculum delivery. In the middle and longer term, several other possibilities are available:

Reduce teaching to the test

The evaluation reports indicate that, in the very pressured circumstances of their work, Early Years teachers were in some ways 'teaching to the test' and the Warwick study expresses concern about this. The broader 'level descriptions' of the new National Curriculum should help to reduce this and to make teaching more responsive to children's needs and development.

Resolve the discrepancies

The evaluation studies provide considerable evidence of Early Years teachers retaining a clear sense of priority in curriculum planning in the midst of what felt like a whirlwind of change over which they had little control (Evans *et al.* 1994: 225). Despite a general feeling that the time devoted to the teaching of reading has declined, long-term comparative studies suggest that this may not be the case (Plewis and Veltman 1994). Nevertheless, the evaluation studies did also throw up several discrepancies, where teachers' reports were not borne out by observations, for example:

- the balance between teaching English as a subject in itself and through the content of other subjects

- the balance between group and individual teaching in the teaching of spelling and handwriting
- the teaching of phonics as isolated exercises, when research suggests that such teaching is most effective when done in the context of continuous text (including text which celebrates the 'word play' possibilities of English) (Adams 1990).

Check the technical terms

The evaluation studies also indicated that the new National Curriculum makes certain technical references whose precise meaning seems not to be widely known. An example is the knowledge that standard English is a dialect, comprising established vocabulary and grammatical rules; it can be spoken in a variety of accents, regional and the non-regional 'R.P.' (once 'received with pleasure' at Court). Other examples include assumptions about onset and rime, the parts of syllables (e.g. in the word sing) which can be developed into alliteration (*s*-ing; *s*-et; *s*-ong) and into rhymes (s-*ing*; br-*ing*; str-*ing*). Awareness of onsets and rimes seems to be an interim stage of children's growing knowledge of the sound system of English (its phonology), coming between awareness of syllables and awareness of the discrete speech sounds or phonemes (/s/i/ng/) on which phonics teaching is predominantly based. This area of professional studies provides an interesting interaction between the worlds of linguistics, psychology, literature and Early Years teaching (Beard 1995).

Keep an eye on research findings

Although the new National Curriculum may be more comprehensive than its predecessor, it will obviously not provide all the insights and support which are necessary for the delivery of a broad and balanced curriculum. Commercial materials will play their part in providing support, but research findings help to give their use an additional edge. Several examples have already been mentioned. In addition, Rosemary Sassoon's (1990) work on handwriting gives detailed advice on the teaching of this important 'key skill'. Several books give research-based directions for the teaching of spelling, including the shift from 'invented' spelling to conventional spelling (e.g. Mudd 1993). Several interesting new publications bring together a variety of helpful ideas on early literacy (e.g. Bielby 1994; Clark 1994).

Such strategies point to insights into how the implementation of the new National Curriculum in English may be evaluated and to the kinds of professional understanding on which effective teaching can be based.

REFERENCES

Adams, M.J. (1990) *Beginning to Read*. Cambridge, MA: MIT Press.

Bald, J. (1993) Rebuilt better than new. *Times Educational Supplement*, 10 December: 25.

Beard, R. (ed.) (1995) *Rhyme, Reading and Writing*. London: Hodder and Stoughton.

Beard, R. and Oakhill, J. (1994) *Reading by Apprenticeship?* Slough: NFER.

Bielby, N. (1994) *Making Sense of Reading*. Leamington Spa: Scholastic Publications Ltd.

Cato, V., Fernandes, C., Gorman, T., Kispal, A. with White, J. (1992) *The Teaching of Early Literacy: How Do Teachers Do It?* Slough: NFER.

Clark, M.M. (1994) *Young Literacy Learners*. Leamington Spa: Scholastic Publications Ltd.

Clay, M.M. (1966) cited in Teale, W. and Sulzby, E. (1986) *Emergent Literacy: Writing and Reading*. Norwood, NJ: Lawrence Erlbaum Associates.

DES (1989) *English in the National Curriculum*. London: HMSO.

Evans, L., Packwood, A., Neill, S.R. St.J. and Campbell, R.J. (1994) *The Meaning of Infant Teachers' Work*. London: Routledge.

Gorman, T. and Fernandes, C. (1992) *Reading in Recession*. Slough: NFER.

Mudd, N. (1993) *Effective Spelling*. London: Hodder and Stoughton.

NCC (1991) *Report on the Monitoring the Implementation of the National Curriculum Core Subjects 1989–90*. York: NCC.

NCC (1992) *National Curriculum English: The Case for Revising the Order*. York: National Curriculum Council.

Perera, K. (1993) The good book: linguistic aspects, in Beard, R. (ed.) *Teaching Literacy: Balancing Perspectives*. London: Hodder and Stoughton.

Plewis, I. and Veltman, M. (1994) Where Does All the Time Go? Changes in Infant Pupils' Experiences Since the Education Reform Act. Paper presented to British Association Conference, 6 September.

Raban, B., Clark, U. and McIntyre, J. (1994) *Evaluation of the Implementation of English in the National Curriculum at Key Stages 1, 2 and 3 (1991–1993): Final Report*. London: School Curriculum and Assessment Authority.

Sassoon, R. (1990) *Handwriting: The Way to Teach It*. Cheltenham: Stanley Thornes.

3 MATHEMATICS

Ann MacNamara

The National Curriculum was introduced in order to challenge expectations and to raise standards; to broaden the range of subjects studied in the primary classroom and to guarantee that all children irrespective of the school they attend, should be taught the same body of essential knowledge, understanding and skills.

(NCC 1993: para. 1.1)

This chapter will explore to what degree this has happened in relation to Mathematics at Key Stage One. The state of Mathematics teaching and learning immediately before and during the introduction of the National Curriculum will be discussed. The chapter will then consider some of the influences of its introduction on teachers in Key Stage One and the ways in which it is likely to affect the teaching and learning of Mathematics in the future.

THE NATURE OF THE MATHEMATICS CURRICULUM

The Cockcroft Report (DES 1982: 67) stated that teachers perceived Mathematics as 'difficult to teach and to learn'; and many of them expressed doubt as to their own abilities in the subject. There are teachers still in post who did not need to have passed GCE in order to enter Teacher Training Colleges. Few specialized in Mathematics in their College or University course or even at 'A' level. Many are now competent teachers of Mathematics, having developed a strong sense of the need to understand Mathematics in order to be able to do it, to enjoy doing it and to teach it to others; some, however, still have a fear of Mathematics and would say that they are not 'good' at it. About a third of Key Stage One teachers say that they need some help with Mathematics (Wragg *et al.* 1989; Croll and Moses 1990; Bennett *et al.* 1992). These teachers need to be supported and extended in their own understanding and knowledge of Mathematics in order to support their teaching of the subject.

Major changes in the Mathematics taught in primary schools had begun in the 1960s with the introduction of the Nuffield Mathematics project. The materials produced emphasized the pupil's active learning in Mathematics and the development of a wider curriculum than the previous arithmetic-led primary Mathematics curriculum. The Plowden Report (CACE 1967) had emphasized that children learned to think mathematically by doing Mathematics, but had pointed out the dangers of the new approach becoming formalized '. . . we must emphasise that the last thing we wish to see is a hardening of the new approach into an accepted syllabus supported by textbooks, work books and commercially produced apparatus and consecrated by familiarity' (CACE 1967: para. 662).

The Cockcroft Report built upon this beginning and there was a gradual change in the nature of the Mathematics taught in schools. This was encouraged by two changes: firstly, by the demise of the 11 + examination and the resultant change in the assessment/examination dominated curriculum of the last two years of the primary school; and secondly, by the introduction of advisory teachers who supported the changes in Mathematics teaching through LEA in-service courses and work alongside teachers in the classroom. OFSTED noted in their report of 1994 on Science and Mathematics teaching that, 'A broadening of the mathematics curriculum resulted but, as an inevitable consequence, the learning time devoted to proficiency in basic arithmetic was reduced' (OFSTED 1994: 16).

The introduction of the National Curriculum 'held out the promise of a radical transformation of the primary curriculum' (Campbell and Neill 1994). The 14 attainment targets of the original Mathematics Order broadened Mathematics teaching, introducing aspects of Mathematics that had not been taught before in many schools. At first, the National Curriculum was accepted by almost all teachers in Key Stage One; it was only when the implications of the assessment procedures and the realization of the work-load for both teachers and children became clear, that there was disagreement about its feasibility.

The National Curriculum Mathematics Order is based on certain interlocking assumptions about the nature of Mathematics – perceived as a utilitarian subject – and the teaching and learning process. The first is that Mathematics learning can be organized in a hierarchical manner, the notion of levels presupposing that there is an order in which Mathematics should be taught and learnt. The second is that Mathematics can be broken down into discrete areas, even in the early stages of learning. The third is that a level in one area of the Programme of Study is equivalent to the same level in another area, both in terms of conceptual difficulty and age appropriateness. A further consideration is that a level in Mathematics is supposed to be 'equivalent' to the same level in other subjects 'As the same scale applies to all areas of study you will be able to compare ... performance across the whole range of National Curriculum subjects' (DES 1989b).

A concern which has arisen since the Dearing Review (1994) is that the Key Stage One Programme of Study limits the children to Levels 1 to 3 within each of the areas of Mathematics unless the children are taught from the Key Stage Two Programmes of Study. To quote Clemson and Clemson (1994: 81), these levels 'look like limits, not opportunities'.

At Key Stage One, many teachers have regarded Mathematics as a separate subject, mainly computation, taught apart from the rest of the curriculum. This approach has been ratified, sanctified almost, by the format of the National Curriculum, which was itself produced in distinct subject sections, written by subject teams who did not collaborate with each other. In policy documents, the National Curriculum Council talks about a 'subject approach' (DES 1989b: 3.1.ii). Many Key Stage One teachers believed that the National Curriculum had been written and devised from the perspective of GCSE in Mathematics with the corresponding notion that, for the younger child, the Mathematics curriculum should have the same basic structure but less content.

QUALITY OF WORK

Concern about the standard of Mathematics teaching, learning and attainment is not new; the Chief HMI, reporting in 1989 on

Standards in Education for 1988–9, reported that 90 per cent of the basic skills work in primary Mathematics was satisfactory or better, but that the picture deteriorated markedly when more advanced mathematical skills and applications were considered and he suggested that the balance of work needed to be wider. Other research (DES 1978, 1982, 1985; Bennett 1984; Tizard *et al.* 1988; Alexander 1992) has indicated that there was a great emphasis on the teaching and learning of the basic understanding of number in the infant school, with little other Mathematics. There was a 'heavy concentration of time on basics of number ... often presented through routine exercises and drills' (Campbell and Neill 1994: 2). As OFSTED (1994) pointed out, although most pupils could perform the basic arithmetical skills adequately if they knew which operation to apply, they had difficulties when the problem was in context, when they were unsure which operation to use.

Pre-National Curriculum, concern had been expressed that the influence of the introduction of Mathematics schemes had led to a rise in the amount of workcard-led Mathematics, where the children, although sitting in groups in the classroom, were in fact working individually. Bennett, in observing 6 and 7-year-olds in infant classrooms, noted, 'Most effort was spent on producing features of tasks rather than on progression through an exercise, manifested in copying, rubbing out, boxing answers and the like' (1989: 112).

Difficulties in getting the right match for the children had been noted earlier by Bennett *et al.* (1984: 113) see Table 1 (where the attainment is the attainment of the pupil as noted by the teacher and the tasks set were monitored by HMI). Overall, the fact that less than half of the children observed were working on materials matched to their abilities was of great concern; the range of difficulty of the materials provided was not wide enough to cover the needs of the high attainers and the low attainers.

Since the introduction of the National Curriculum, the match of work to children's abilities seems to have improved. OFSTED (1993: 12) report that 'a quarter of the more able pupils were engaged in tasks which were too easy for them. A quarter of the work set to the less able pupils was too difficult and prevented them succeeding. Generally, three-fifths of all pupils were successful in work that was pitched at an appropriate level of difficulty'. The problem of match is exacerbated at Key Stage One by the high level of reading demanded of the children before they can engage with the Mathematics. Often, children find it difficult to understand the

Table 1 Matching the level of difficulty in children's work with their ability

Attainment	Match %	Too easy %	Too hard %
High	41	41	16
Average	43	26	26
Low	44	12	25

Source: N. Bennett *et al.* (1984).

problem because they are not able to read or fully understand the language used, even though the Mathematics itself is at a lower level of difficulty.

TIME ON MATHEMATICS

The amount of time that children spend 'doing' Mathematics varies from class to class and school to school. It is difficult to define exactly what it is that is meant by 'doing mathematics'. Before the introduction of the National Curriculum, the Cockcroft Report recommended that primary children should spend between four and five hours a week on designated Mathematics, with some Mathematics being done outside this time (para. 104) presumably on topic-related work. After the introduction of the National Curriculum, Campbell and Neill (1994) found an average of 6.7 hours; but as Alexander *et al.* (1992) pointed out, time used less efficiently – with less work and more distractions – undermines the assumption that quality depends directly upon time allocated to Mathematics.

The recommendations from the DES, that 20 per cent of the time in an 18-hour teaching week should be spent on Mathematics, would allow for 3.6 hours of Mathematics per week, and, in terms of manageability '. . . [the] only workable strategy is for substantial elements of . . . Mathematics to be consciously planned, delivered and assessed through their applications in other subjects' (Campbell and Neill 1994: 33).

It is difficult to isolate exactly how much time children spend doing Mathematics in Key Stage One, partly because of the difficulty of defining what is meant by the terms. Also the nature of classroom organization at Key Stage One, where children may work in groups in a carousel system with four or more activities going on at the same time and when activities may be chosen from a menu, confounds the problem. From Campbell's survey, it appears that, over the five years of the National Curriculum, the amount of time spent on Mathematics in Key Stage One as a percentage of the time spent on all subjects fell from 20 per cent in 1990 to 18 per cent in 1993. Nevertheless, three-quarters of the teachers interviewed thought that there was enough time for Mathematics. In terms of how the Mathematics time was divided between the different aspects of Mathematics, OFSTED reported that 'number work is appropriately emphasised in schools . . . but that the use of this time was poor and excessive time spent on number was a more serious obstacle to progress than lack of time' (OFSTED 1994: 20). The implication here was that enough time was spent on the basics of arithmetical competence, but it was not being used effectively.

The introduction of the National Curriculum in Mathematics and the lack of time for Mathematics influenced some teachers (Mac-Namara 1994) to comment that they were now thinking much more about the methods and organization that they were using to teach Mathematics.

CONTENT

In terms of the content taught, the National Curriculum has broadened the Mathematics curriculum. Now, in Key Stage One classes, children are taught the foundations of algebra, an appreciable amount of geometry, some data handling and some elements of probability; although the last is to be moved into Key Stage Two with the Dearing revisions. Tackling these aspects of Mathematics has been difficult for those teachers who are not confident in the subject. The problem was that teachers did not have a wide enough knowledge of Mathematics to give them the confidence to allow children to explore Mathematics in a truly open sense. Lack of knowledge can lead teachers to make generalized statements to children that were not mathematically correct: for instance, 'multiplication makes things bigger'.

Ironically it is teaching about number, where teachers feel most confident, which is described by OFSTED (1994: 21) as 'the area of greatest need'. In-service courses offered by Higher Education and LEAs on number are often the least popular as teachers feel they do not need to come on them because they have been teaching number for many years.

The inclusion of Attainment Target 1, 'Using and Applying Mathematics', in the National Curriculum – and its retention after the Dearing Review – encouraged teachers to become aware of the benefits of teaching children in an open and investigative manner. There is now more emphasis on problem solving which has made Mathematics work in the classroom more interesting, encouraging pupils to think more for themselves. This should help to improve children's basic competence in Mathematics, for as Desforges and Cockburn (1987: 3) said '. . . children do not need further doses of basic skills training . . . they need to learn to think with mathematics rather than merely respond with routines'.

COMMERCIAL SCHEMES OF WORK

Before the introduction of the National Curriculum, concern was being expressed about the role and influence of commercial schemes of work in Mathematics. The *Assessment of Achievement Programme* asked 'Are pupils spending too much time passively contemplating worksheets and written examples without a balance of real tasks in which to develop mathematical understanding?' (Scottish Education Department 1988: 9.8xii). This concern was echoed by the DES report which said there was '. . . little evidence to suggest that heavy reliance on routine sessions of mathematics based on textbooks and published work cards resulted in the most effective learning . . .' (1989a: para. 24).

Since the introduction of the National Curriculum, there have been many more published schemes of work advertised to cover all the Attainment Targets. HMI and later OFSTED have been consistent in their concerns about the use of these schemes: 'Many schools used a commercial mathematics scheme, and . . . there was undue reliance on them in most schools' (DES 1990: para. 24); 'The quality of work varied according to the way the teachers used these (commercial) texts . . . The rigid adherence to one scheme did not adequately provide the content required by the National Curriculum' (DES 1993: para. 23); 'a third of classes place an over-reliance on a particular published scheme and this led to pupils spending prolonged periods of time on repetitive and undemanding exercises which did little to advance their skill or understanding, much less their interest and enthusiasm' (OFSTED 1994: 23).

However, one teacher interviewed recently (MacNamara 1994), suggested that pre-National Curriculum work was very scheme based as there was no other framework; now that the National Curriculum provides the syllabus, scheme books are used as a resource. Certainly, this was in evidence in her school although it would appear that it is not so everywhere.

One of the effects of the National Curriculum may have been to introduce children to the Mathematics scheme at an earlier age. The use of workcards and individualized learning packages has meant that many younger children are now using scheme materials for much of their Mathematics learning. The dangers in this include the difficulty that young children have in reading the instructions on the worksheet, despite the limited mathematical demand of the work. Making the language simple enough for a beginning reader often means that the mathematical demand is too simple for the children, although the total cognitive demand of decoding the instructions is too great. There is a real problem of match here. Another problem is that most schemes are designed for the child to use as an individual, so that elements of cooperative learning have to be deliberately built into the organization of learning experiences in the classroom.

This is not to imply that commercial schemes of work have no place in the Early Years Mathematics curriculum; many of them provide a wealth of materials for children to use, with structured activities that can offer opportunities for practice of basic skills through games and other activities. Some of them provide topic areas from which mathematical activities can be devised, others offer opportunities for children to extend their experiences; but none of them can offer the quality of mathematical education that a confident and interested teacher can provide.

An unintended side effect of the wholesale introduction of commercial schemes to cover all the work for Key Stage One has been to undermine the confidence of the class teacher. Rarely do the schemes address the fact that the teacher may well disagree with the statements made, or want to change the order of material introduced. The implication is that the scheme has been written by 'experts' and as such should be followed slavishly by the teacher. In many cases, the teacher does not feel that they have enough confidence to change it; but a scheme, even if written and trialled

Schemes ?

extensively with a group of children, will still need alteration and adaptation for use with any other child or class in order to gain the most benefit from it.

Most Mathematics schemes are designed for children to work through independently and scheme questions are rarely open-ended. They do not allow for the children to explore and to act like mathematicians. This encourages children to believe that all Mathematics consists of questions which are able to be solved and to which there is only one correct answer. Many children see school Mathematics as getting the answers correct and reaching the end of the scheme book so that they can get on to the next one. Often, the children can complete pages of 'sums' in their workbooks (and get them 'right') without any real understanding of the Mathematics involved. Evidence of this is found in the ease with which children can 'do' sums – that is, perform written calculations – but then not apply this skill to real life problems (Threlfall 1992; OFSTED 1994; Thumpston 1994).

ASSESSMENT

Pre-National Curriculum, most formal assessment in Mathematics had concentrated upon children's understanding of number with either teacher-designed or standardized NFER or Richmond tests. These were norm referenced either formally, as in the case of NFER or informally, as in the case of the teacher-designed tests. Other assessment was designed by the teacher to support diagnosis or to evaluate the teaching programme, 'to support the development of the learner' (Thumpston 1994: 111).

With the introduction of the National Curriculum came Standard Assessment Tasks (SATs), which were designed to be part of a total assessment package. The original SATs for Key Stage One were developed so that some of the Statements of Attainment (SoAs) assessed were based on current classroom themes. SoAs which could not be assessed in that way were done separately. The SATs at that time were intended to 'allow students opportunities to be questioned and to respond in a variety of modes – oral, written, practical and pictorial' (Joffe 1992: 206). The vast number of SoAs to be assessed over a short period of time in English, Mathematics and Science with classes of up to 35 children made this an impossible task – 'too complex . . . too cumbersome . . . too expensive' (ibid.: 244). The resultant changes in curriculum – 14 Attainment Targets in Mathematics down to 5 and now, post-Dearing, down to 3 – have been matched by a reduction of assessment modes to formal pencil and paper assessment mainly based on number. Whether this narrowing of the formal assessment will lead to a further narrowing of the curriculum as teachers concentrate most on mathematics which is formally assessed is not yet known. Publication of these results will put pressure upon schools who wish to retain the breadth of the curriculum in Mathematics.

Teacher assessment – originally designed to offer 60 per cent of the final pupil assessment – changed (rapidly) to 40 per cent (ibid.: 207) and is now (post-Dearing) to stand alongside the SAT score as a separate measure. As there was no 'official' model offered, teachers have developed their own model of teacher assessment related to their own philosophy. This has been mainly norm referenced because this is where teachers have most expertise. As McCallum says, 'Teacher Assessment of the National Curriculum has been particularly difficult for infant teachers because of the lack of training and support materials' (McCallum 1993: 332).

In the first few years of the National Curriculum, teachers were given conflicting advice by their LEAs and the Schools Examination and Assessment Council (SEAC) about the amount of pupil material they had to keep in order to have their judgements moderated. Some teachers were keeping and formally assessing all the written work that the children were doing with the resultant overload of both time and space. Teachers felt that the results were used to judge their teaching. The assessment was 'fervent but unfocused' (Campbell and Neill 1994: 42). Of the Key Stage One teachers interviewed in the PACE study 55 per cent said that they had changed their teaching methods as a result of carrying out National Curriculum assessment.

Teacher assessment is a skill which teachers have to learn; it is difficult to step back and make an assessment of a pupil's work without helping them. Teachers need training to be good assessors and training to moderate other teachers' assessments, otherwise there will not be consistency in teacher assessment across the country. Unless this happens, teacher assessment will not be given the weight that it deserves.

However, assessment that is carried out with young children by means of pencil and paper tests will, of necessity, be limited to the assessment of a narrow band of Mathematics. A formal test – for that is what the Key Stage One mathematics SAT is – can only sample a small amount of the knowledge, skills and understanding of the child. It would be detrimental to Mathematics education if the effect of the National Curriculum was constrained by the requirements of formal assessment. It is crucial that the role of teacher assessment is seen as having equal standing as the SAT in order to provide evidence of a young child's achievement.

MATHEMATICS AT KEY STAGE ONE: THE WAY FORWARD

Stability in terms of the curriculum content, which is now promised for the next five years, should enable Key Stage One teachers to consolidate the work that they have achieved in Mathematics.

In the OFSTED report on the implementation of the National Curriculum (1993), it was reported that the overall quality of the work in mathematics in Key Stage One was significantly better than in the 1991–2 sample. But in 1994, OFSTED said that 'The National Curriculum is improving teaching rapidly and must be given a chance . . . Immediate benefit would be seen if teachers' confidence in their own mathematical competence could be improved' (1994: 22). The fact that teachers do not feel confident is echoed throughout the literature: 'The trend is for teachers to feel less competent now, sometimes markedly so' (Bennett *et al.* 1992: 61); 'Inspection shows that the attitudes of many . . . teachers have steadily and gradually become less positive as they have shouldered the burden of the changes to the National Curriculum' (OFSTED 1994: 36); 'The problems appear to lie with the teachers' own confidence in mathematics' (ibid.: 21); 'Teachers are losing confidence in their own professionalism and feeling undervalued' (Key Stage One teacher, cited in MacNamara 1994). These are significant statements and must be considered by the government if there is to be a real improvement in Mathematics teaching.

There are well established ways of developing teacher confidence and competence in Mathematics; amongst them are 20-day courses in Mathematics. These have been carefully evaluated and demonstrably successful (Kinder *et al.* 1991; Harland and Kinder 1992). Teachers are very willing to attend these longer courses as part of their professional development but they cannot any longer be funded out of existing school budgets. Part of the cost must come from central government.

Key Stage One teachers have improved their teaching of Mathematics with the National Curriculum. They would all agree that this could be improved further. They would see the need for time to reflect on ways of teaching and assessing Mathematics. The role of the advisory teachers in supporting Mathematics teaching was seminal; it is ironic that the virtual demise of the advisory teacher and the change of role of the advisor to inspector should have happened at a time when they could have been most valuable in supporting teachers in their judgements about pupils' work (OFSTED 1994).

The next generation of teachers will have spent much more time in the classroom as part of their initial training. If, in future, there are to be well-trained, competent teachers, then support must be given to qualified teachers to enable them to feel confident and be competent in mathematics teaching so that they can support and guide their students. In the light of the teachers' attempts to make the National Curriculum work, government support in terms of a commitment to a programme of in-service training would be more than welcome.

REFERENCES

Alexander, R., Rose, J. and Woodhead, C. (1992) *Curriculum Organisation and Classroom Practice in Primary Schools*. London: DES.

Bennett, N., Desforges, C., Cockburn, A. and Wilkinson, B. (1984) *Quality of Pupil Learning Experiences*. London: Lawrence Erlbaum.

Bennett, N. (1989) Teaching and learning Mathematics in the primary school, in P. Ernest (ed.) *Mathematics Teaching; the State of the Art*. Brighton: Falmer Press.

Bennett, S.N., Wragg, E.C., Carré, C.G. and Carter, D.S.G. (1992) A longitudinal study of primary teachers' perceived competences in, and concerns about, National Curriculum implementation, *Research Papers in Education*, 7: 53–78.

CACE (Central Advisory Council for Education (1967) *Children and Their Primary Schools* (The Plowden Report). London: HMSO.

Campbell, R.J., Neill, S.R. St.J. (1994) *Curriculum Reform at Key Stage 1; Teacher Commitment and Policy Failure*. London: Longman Information and Reference.

Clemson, D. and Clemson, W. (1994) *Mathematics in the Early Years*. London: Routledge.

Croll, P. and Moses, D. (1990) Perspectives on the National Curriculum in Primary and Secondary Schools, *Educational Studies*, 16(2): 187–98.

Dearing, R. (1994) *The National Curriculum and its Assessment: Final Report*. London: SCAA.

DES (1978) *Primary Education in England; A Survey by HM Inspectors of Schools*. London: HMSO.

DES (1982) *Mathematics Counts* (The Cockcroft Report). London: HMSO.

DES (1985) *Mathematics from 5 to 16: Curriculum Matters 3; An HMI Series*. London: HMSO.

DES (1989a) *Mathematics in the National Curriculum*. London: HMSO.

DES (1989b) *The National Curriculum – A Guide for Parents of Primary Children*. York: NCC.

DES (1990) *Mathematics Key Stages 1 and 3*. London: HMSO.

Desforges, C. and Cockburn, A. (1987) *Understanding the Mathematics Teacher*. Brighton: Falmer Press.

Harland, J. and Kinder, K. (1992) *Mathematics and Science Courses for Primary Teachers*. Windsor: NFER.

Joffe, L.S. (1992) The English experience of a National Curriculum and assessments, in G. Leder (ed.) *Assessment and Learning of Mathematics*. Australia: ACER.

Kinder, K., Harland, J. and Wootten, M. (1991) *The Impact of School Focused INSET on Classroom Practice*. Windsor: NFER.

McCallum, B. (1993) Teacher assessment at Key Stage One. *Research Papers in Education*, 8(3): 305–27.

MacNamara, E.A. (1994) 'Primary Teachers' Reflections on the First Five Years', unpublished article. University of Leeds.

OFSTED (Office for Standards in Education) (1993a) *Mathematics Key Stages 1, 2 and 3*. London: HMSO.

OFSTED (1993b) *Mathematics Key Stages 1, 2, 3 and 4*. London: HMSO.

OFSTED (1994) *Science and Mathematics in Schools*. London: HMSO.

Pollard, A., Broadfoot, P., Croll, P., Osborn, M. and Abbott, D. (1994) *Changing English Primary Schools*. London: Cassell.

Scottish Education Department (1988) *Assessment of Achievement Programme (Mathematics)*. Edinburgh: HMSO.

Threlfall, J. (1992) No sums, please, we're infants. *Education 3–13*, 20(2): 15–17.

Thumpston, G. (1994) Mathematics in the National Curriculum; implications for learning in the early years, in G.M. Blenkin and A.V. Kelly (eds) *The National Curriculum and Early Learning: An Evaluation*. London: Paul Chapman Publications.

Tizard, B., Blatchford, P., Burke, J., Farquar, C. and Plewis, I. (1988) *Young Children at School in the Inner City*. London: Lawrence Erlbaum.

Wragg, E.C., Bennett, S.N. and Carré, C.G. (1989) Primary teachers and the National Curriculum. *Research Papers in Education*, 4: 17–37.

4	SCIENCE
	Hilary Asoko

INTRODUCTION

Children arriving in school already have considerable experience of events and phenomena in the natural world. They have expectations of how things behave and express surprise when these expectations are violated. They also have some understanding of cause and effect and are developing a vocabulary which includes words used in Science such as force, light, energy, animal, though these words are associated with their everyday, rather than their scientific, meanings. Children are curious about the world around them and are continually attempting to reconcile information received from sensory experience with ideas obtained from a range of other sources – adults, other children, books, television – as well as with their own previous knowledge. They have ideas about some of the phenomena and events which are of interest to Science. Sometimes these ideas, though embryonic, are consistent with the scientific view and could be developed or extended. On the other hand ideas may be very different from the scientific view. Frequently, children simply take things for granted: when a bonfire burns, a large heap of garden rubbish is reduced to a small pile of ash; shining a torch on a wall produces a bright spot; metal spoons sink but metal ships float. What happens to the 'stuff' when the bonfire burns? How does the spot of light get on the wall? What makes the ship float? These questions may not occur to the child – such phenomena are not seen as odd or needing explanation.

Young children are quite able to *describe* a range of everyday events – it goes dark every night, washing dries on the line, things fall when you drop them. They may give *reasons* for what happens in terms of their personal relationship to the particular event – it goes dark at night so that we can sleep, the washing dries so we can wear clean clothes, the ball falls because you let go. However, a scientific *explanation* draws upon concepts which the child has not yet encountered – the earth spinning in front of a stationary sun, water changing state from liquid to gas and becoming part of the air, an invisible force called gravity pulling the ball without touching it. Such ideas can provide powerful ways of looking at, thinking about and interacting with the world. Are we helping young children to start developing them?

Estimates of time spent teaching Science in Key Stage One classes range from 10 to 15 per cent (OFSTED 1993b). Teachers spend hours producing plans, monitoring and assessing children's progress and keeping records. The choice of equipment and resources available to support teaching is ever increasing. At any time during the school week, young children can be found 'doing science' – lighting bulbs by wiring them to batteries, sorting materials into groups, recording whether objects float or sink in water, planting seeds in different conditions, carrying out a variety of 'fair tests'. Such activities, and many others like them, certainly seem like Science, but are they being used to maximum effect?

It is clear that the *quantity* of teaching which is identified as Science has increased in recent years, but what of the *quality* of the childrens' learning? This chapter will explore the current situation in Early Years classrooms and how it has arisen, as well as considering how we might develop and improve Science teaching and learning in the future.

REVIEWING THE PAST

In 1978, according to a survey undertaken by Her Majesty's Inspectorate and despite major curriculum projects such as Nuffield Junior Science (1967) and Science 5–13 (Schools Council 1972), only one primary class in ten was receiving a satisfactory Science curriculum, little experimental work or work in the physical sciences was occurring and in some schools there was no Science teaching at all (DES 1978). HMI reported 11 years later that all but one of 300 schools inspected between 1982 and 1986 included Science in the curriculum but considered that both the time spent, on average about 5 per cent of the total teaching time available, and the depth of work were disappointing. The quality of work observed was judged good or better in about one-third of classes whilst in one-fifth it was considered poor (DES 1989a). For younger children Science was usually taught through topic work and biological science predominated. Some teachers provided 'interest tables' with equipment such as magnets or magnifying glasses or considered they were including Science through play with water, sand or construction materials.

During the 1980s support for class teachers to develop Science teaching came from central government initiatives. Between 1984 and 1987 over 1,350 science coordinators attended 35-day training courses. These were often blocked in 2 or 3-day units across the school year. From 1985, Education Support Grants provided LEAs with resources which were often used to appoint advisory teachers, who worked alongside teachers in their own classrooms as well as organizing in-service activities. Whilst 'primary science was an area of the curriculum about which many primary practitioners held deep reservations, and one which they often readily admitted they neither liked nor understood' (Kinder and Harland 1991: 127) the impending arrival of the National Curriculum, specified by the Education Reform Act of 1988, meant that teachers had to reconsider their position with respect to Science. From September 1989, when the National Curriculum first came into effect in Year One classrooms, Science was officially regarded as a core subject with the same status as English or Mathematics, two areas in which teachers of Early Years children had traditionally concentrated both their time and their efforts.

Few of these teachers, however, had a strong personal background in Science, the majority being female non-graduates with an arts or humanities background and at least ten years classroom experience (Wragg *et al.* 1989; Bennett *et al.* 1992). When primary school pupils themselves, they were likely to have experienced little, if any, Science teaching and many of them would have finished their formal education in Science at or before the age of 16. Attitudes, especially to the physical sciences, were less than positive. Based on their own, often unhappy, experiences from secondary school, many teachers associated Science with Bunsen burners, test-tubes, and a body of knowledge which was not only difficult to understand but apparently unrelated or irrelevant to everyday life. A sample of 901 primary teachers, surveyed in 1989, revealed that only 34 per cent felt competent to teach Science, compared to 68 per cent and 81 per cent for Mathematics and English respectively (Wragg *et al.* 1989). In the same survey, teachers were asked to assess their competence to teach to specific Statements of Attainment in the National Curriculum. For many of these items, including those on forces, shadows, electricity and scientific investigations, fewer than half the teachers felt competent with their existing knowledge. Teachers' concerns about their lack of knowledge were justified. The Primary School Teachers and Science Project, set up in 1988, surveyed more than 450 primary teachers and found that 'the majority of primary teachers in the sample . . . hold views of Science concepts that are not in accord with those accepted by scientists' (Summers 1992: 26). Nevertheless, studies such as those carried out by the Primary Assessment Curriculum and Experience (PACE) project (Pollard *et al.* 1994) report that Early Years teachers were not opposed to the introduction of the National Curriculum in principle; indeed, many welcomed the guidelines and structure it provided.

Those, such as advisory teachers for Science, who were involved in preparing teachers for the introduction of the National Curriculum and supporting them in the early stages, tended to minimize the enormity of the task, and thus the anxiety associated with it, by trying to reassure teachers that they were already doing some Science though perhaps not recognizing it as such. Two key messages of the Education Support Grant scheme studied by Kinder and Harland (1991) were identified as the value of teaching Science though topics and the belief that much of the teachers' existing curriculum could be redefined as Science. For many teachers, therefore, the problem became one of first deciding what, from their existing practice, could be labelled as science; second, finding science activities which could fit into existing topics to increase the amount of Science in the curriculum; and finally, 'filling the gaps' in areas which had previously not been covered but which were now required. Short in-service courses frequently focused on these needs rather than on developing either teachers' own knowledge and understanding of Science or on developing a rationale for teaching Science to particular age groups. Thus, although teachers were provided with many practical ideas regarding the teaching of Science they were less well equipped to evaluate activities or to recognize when and how to use them.

Longer courses, such as the 20-day in-service, funded through the

Local Education Authority Training Grants Scheme (LEATGS) and later Grants for Education Support and Training (GEST), were intended to focus on teachers' own subject knowledge as well as enhancing teaching skills in Science and developing strategies for dissemination to colleagues. HMI, reporting on these courses, considered them to be well received by teachers and that 'the standard of . . . science lessons in the course participants' classes was usually somewhat above that of similar lessons in other classes in the school' (DES 1992a: 2). However, given the limited resources to support attendance on such courses, it is a minority of teachers who have had the opportunity to benefit from such training. The extent to which these teachers can influence the work of their colleagues is very variable. 'A common finding was that the course had affected the work of the participants but had little influence on the work of others in the school' (DES 1992a: 4).

The implementation of the curricular requirements of the Act regarding Science have been monitored by HMI and reported annually (DES 1992b; OFSTED 1993a, 1993b). By 1993, 72 per cent of science lessons were judged satisfactory or better at Key Stage One with the time allocated estimated at, on average, 10 to 15 per cent of teaching time, which the inspectors judged 'adequate'.

Teachers' perceptions of changes in the curriculum resulting from the introduction of the National Curriculum, as reported in the PACE study, noted an increase in the amount of science taught. Of the 84 per cent of teachers surveyed in 1990 and the 73 per cent in 1991, it was felt that the subject was being taught 'more' than previously. However, classroom observations from the same study reveal that, as the main curriculum subject, Science was recorded less than 10 per cent of the time, whilst the other core subjects, Mathematics and English, took over 50 per cent of the time between them. Campbell and Neill's study (1994) estimates that the time allocated to Science as a percentage of total teaching time for all subjects in Key Stage One classes was 13 per cent in 1990, peaked at 15 per cent in 1991 and fell to 10 and 9 per cent in 1992 and 1993 respectively. This time allocation was perceived as 'adequate' by 64 per cent of the teachers. The discrepancy between time allocated to Science in comparison to the other core subjects suggests that Science is effectively 'a foundation subject as far as classroom teachers are concerned' (Farrow 1992: 314). By 1993 more than 50 per cent of teachers felt that standards in Science had been raised as a result of the National Curriculum. Whilst few felt that standards had been lowered it is interesting that, despite so much activity, 44 per cent perceived that there had been no effect (Campbell and Neill 1994).

THE CURRENT SITUATION

The Programmes of Study specify both conceptual and procedural understanding of Science. Knowledge and ideas are detailed in Attainment Targets 2–4, whilst Attainment Target 1 relates to scientific ways of working. Whatever teachers' feelings about teaching Science before the introduction of the National Curriculum, there is now almost unanimous agreement that it is an appropriate part of the Early Years curriculum. What then are their views on its purpose and what does the Science they teach look like?

Most teachers perceive young children to be naturally inquisitive and curious. They see the purpose of Science for this age group largely in terms of stimulating such characteristics and providing opportunities for children to explore and investigate the world around them and this is frequently viewed as an end in itself. Thus Attainment Target 1, 'Exploration of Science' in the original version of the National Curriculum, changed, in 1991, to 'Scientific Investigation' in the revised document and now 'Experimental and Investigative Science' following the Dearing Review (1994), is the part of the National Curriculum which many teachers have felt most able to tackle. Processes such as observing, classifying and investigating are now, retrospectively, identified by teachers as aspects of Science which they included in their teaching prior to the introduction of the National Curriculum. 'Fair testing', which has received a great deal of attention, both in published schemes and through in-service courses, has been incorporated relatively easily into the repertoire of most Early Years teachers. In addition, teachers' perceptions of their personal competence to teach Science has increased, in particular with respect to scientific processes (Bennett *et al.* 1992). The demands on teachers' own knowledge and understanding of scientific concepts is reduced by considering scientific understanding as something which can be discovered by careful observation and investigation of events and phenomena in the natural world.

This view fits comfortably with the beliefs of many teachers about education in the Early Years, which has been summarized by OFSTED 'Briefly stated, "learning by doing" was preferred to "teaching by telling". The view that the primary classroom should provide "active learning experiences" and that teaching should have a practical bias was widespread particularly in Key Stage One' (OFSTED 1993c: 8). Thus, much Early Years Science teaching at the present time is characterized by the provision of activities which provide children with opportunities to explore, investigate, observe and, to a lesser extent, measure in a range of contexts, light sources, magnets, living things, materials, etc. These contexts have been selected from Attainment Targets 2, 3 and 4 and may form part of a cross-curricular topic such as 'Journeys' or 'Ourselves' or a Science-focused topic, for example 'Materials'. Children are encouraged to ask questions and try to find ways to answer them, frequently by using 'fair tests'. The emphasis on 'hands-on' practical activities allows teachers who are unsure of the Science to see themselves as 'discovering' scientific concepts with the children. The teaching emphasis is on the *process* of Science at the expense of scientific knowledge and understanding which has 'to a large extent been marginalised in practice' (Feasey 1994: 76).

There is an underlying assumption that by giving children opportunities to interact with objects and phenomena, they will learn Science. Official documents, such as the *Science Non-Statutory Guidance* (DES 1989b) have, to an extent, legitimized this view: 'Pupils learn through active engagement in learning experiences and these are outlined in the Programmes of Study. As a result of this engagement, they develop both knowledge and understanding in the area being explored and also their competence in ways of finding out' (A7); 'Conceptual understanding can develop through continuous, well planned, practical experiences' (C2). For many teachers 'active' is equated with 'hands-on'. Thus statements such as these may be interpreted as meaning that *all* that is required for children to learn Science is hands-on activity and the need for teachers to *teach* Science and for learners to be involved in *mental* activity is minimized. If this really is all that is necessary, then we must ask why, after years of such experience, the adult population as a whole, including many primary teachers, has a relatively poor grasp of basic scientific concepts. Clearly experience alone is *not* enough!

It would be helpful for teachers to appreciate that scientific knowledge does not arise simply by 'observing carefully', following a set of prescribed instructions, or collecting and recording data with an empty mind. According to *Science Non-Statutory Guidance* (DES 1989b: A4) 'The scientist chooses from the knowledge and ideas which have been previously established to devise systematic studies into scientific phenomena'. Scientific activity aims to develop or use explanations which are consistent with evidence. The evidence is obtained through structured interactions with objects and phenomena, but the explanations draw upon ideas which are not evident in the object or phenomenon under study but which come from the mind of the observer. Thus, whilst children may be involved in activities concerning such objects and phenomena, it does not necessarily follow that they are doing Science. The activities themselves do not determine whether children use or learn scientific knowledge or operate in a scientific way. It is what is happening mentally when they interact with the activities which matters. In order for children to be truly involved in scientific activity they need access to appropriate ideas and ways of thinking together with opportunities and encouragement to use these ideas. The teacher, therefore, needs not only to provide experiences but also to be prepared to capitalize on the opportunities they provide for introducing, or supporting children in using, 'tools for thinking' in the form of selected scientific ideas and concepts.

However, experience when working with teachers on 20-day in-service courses reveals that they find it difficult to identify the specific concepts which are the focus of their teaching and even more problematic to see how different concepts within a Science topic relate to each other. This means that whilst teachers are now adept at generating activities within specific topics, such as forces or light, they find it difficult to specify the *purpose* of such activities in terms of the opportunities they provide for the introduction or development of scientific concepts. This is a result not only of teachers' insecurity in their own knowledge, to which reference has already been made, but also their lack of experience of children learning Science. 'Primary teachers were less confident in their knowledge about how children's learning develops in Science than they were in Maths and English. This tended to hinder them in developing appropriate science activities or understanding the purpose of activities' (Russell *et al.* 1993: 13). Teachers themselves recognize this dilemma. When asked, on needs based in-service courses, to identify conceptual aims for teaching, teachers admitted to finding it difficult:

> Planning activities comes as second nature to most teachers. What is not always considered is what specific areas of knowledge we are attempting to teach.

Concepts so often get overlooked in the 'rush' of activities and the brainstorming of colleagues in planning meetings.

Primary school teachers have become very good at devising activities to the extent that they lose sight of why they are doing them.

Although thinking about what concepts need developing isn't easy, I have felt that this was what was needed to plan a topic for different levels of ability . . .

Medium to long-term planning tends to focus on what will be 'covered' and is frequently a collaborative venture involving teachers from Reception, and sometimes Nursery, to Year 2. This ensures that everyone knows who will have responsibility for different aspects of the Science curriculum and provides the possibility, at least, of thought being given to the order in which topics, though not usually concepts, are tackled. This type of planning is reflected in the answers teachers give when asked about the Science their class will encounter in the next half term. These are frequently expressed in terms of general statements which are either National Curriculum related, e.g. 'AT2 level 1', 'AT4 strand (ii)', broad conceptual areas such as 'materials', 'life processes' or 'electricity', or, more rarely, are concerned with skills development – observation, predicting or fair testing. The translation of such plans into classroom action tends to remain the responsibility of individuals. Here, activities dominate teacher thinking. These are selected on the basis of past experience of what works in the classroom, seem appropriate for the age group and can be managed and resourced, rather than as part of a long-term considered and coherent strategy which aims to develop children's scientific thinking. Thus, although teachers may be aware of the broad topics being taught by their colleagues and possibly some of the activities to be used, they are much less likely to know what, if any, conceptual focus has been or will be taken and thus the contribution they can make to the overall journey children need to make towards scientific understanding.

Over the years since the introduction of the National Curriculum teachers have learnt, albeit at some cost, to cope with the new roles and responsibilities necessitated by the changes in the nature and extent of Science in the primary school curriculum. Many of them have improved their own knowledge and understanding and most have become familiar with a wider range of activities suitable for the age range. Confidence in managing practically-based activities has increased. Some teachers have recognized the value of discovering how children explain everyday events and phenomena and are developing strategies to carry out formative assessment in the classroom. The challenge is to plan teaching which attempts to confront or build on these explanations and to find ways to introduce children to those scientific concepts which will help them to develop their thinking further. Now that teachers have learnt how to incorporate Science into their classroom routines, the balance can shift from teaching to learning, from coverage to comprehension.

LOOKING TO THE FUTURE

The Dearing Review (1994) and subsequent revision of the National Curriculum Orders mean that significant changes will take effect from September 1995. The time specified as appropriate for Science teaching at Key Stage One, 54 hours per year, is approximately 7 per cent of the total teaching time available, considerably less than for the other core subjects, Mathematics and English. In weekly terms, Science is expected to occupy 1.5 hours, a figure more in line with the 1 hour a week allocated to the foundation subjects than the 3.5 hours for Mathematics or the 5 hours for direct teaching of English. Some schools, therefore, will now reduce the time given to Science as a result of the new Orders. The removal of standard assessments in Science at age 7 squarely places the responsibility for assessment with teachers. On the one hand this appears to devalue the core status of the subject. On the other, it provides the possibility of more emphasis on formative assessment which can be used to inform teaching. The reduction of the content specified by the Orders means that teachers may feel more able to concentrate on specific learning outcomes rather than broad coverage of Science.

The proposed changes respond to Early Years teachers' concerns and recommendations and, although in the short term more work will be generated in restructuring school plans and schemes of work, in the longer term a period of stability, together with a revised curriculum could provide opportunities to develop children's scientific thinking in an effective, coherent and exciting way. However, if this is to happen, it will require all those involved in Science education with young children to ask some important and fundamental questions. Some of these questions, such as those concerned with the aims and purposes of Science education, relate to the Science curriculum as a whole, whilst others are concerned with issues specific to the Early Years. In order to make informed judgements, both about long-term and day-to-day planning, teachers of Early Years children need to consider how the real world and experience of the young child can best be utilized to make new ideas understandable and how the child's world can be extended to encompass new ways of thinking.

This means that teachers need support to enable them to:

- become aware of the words, ideas and ways of thinking typical of this age group and the experiences on which children are likely to draw, which may either help or hinder understanding of Science
- gain access to strategies to find out how the particular children they teach are thinking
- be confident enough in their own understanding of Science to specify clearly the intended learning outcomes for their teaching, to recognize how far along the path towards achieving them children are, and to identify appropriate next steps
- develop the ability to select, design or modify activities which will support children's learning, by developing or challenging their existing ideas and by providing opportunities to introduce appropriate scientific concepts in ways which will make sense to the children
- be aware of helpful ways to interact with children to facilitate this learning. This includes useful questions to ask, ways of focusing attention on salient features, helpful analogies, strategies for explaining which draw upon events and experiences familiar to the children, ways of presenting new ideas and relating these to the child's existing knowledge.

There is an extensive body of research into children's learning of science which would be of benefit to teachers in developing their expertise. Examples include Driver *et al.* (1985), Brook and Driver (1984), Leach *et al.* (1992), SPACE publications (1990–1994). A very useful summary can be found in Driver *et al.* (1994). Curriculum materials such as Nuffield Primary Science (1993) draw upon such research. However, it is true to say that much less is known about children's learning of science in the Early Years than for older pupils. Teachers and researchers together need opportunities to engage in professional debate to identify those concepts which can usefully be introduced to young children and how best to enable them to use these ideas to explore and explain their world in a scientific way.

Of course, it would be ridiculous to expect that the explanations which young children can develop should show the same sophistication or use the same concepts which characterize science. Whilst Newton's laws, particulate theory or evolution seem far removed from the world of the Early Years child, they may be part of the ways of thinking of older pupils or adults. Such ideas do not arise spontaneously and the Early Years education which children receive may start them on the path to developing, understanding and using such explanations. A well-constructed spiral approach to the curriculum can then ensure that concepts introduced during the first years of school can be revisited and developed to greater depth and complexity at later stages in the child's education. Teachers of Early Years children have a crucial role to play, not only in fostering curiosity and a desire to explore and explain but also in helping children to understand the basic concepts from which a scientific view of the world can develop.

REFERENCES

Bennett, S.N., Wragg, E.C., Carré, C.G. and Carter, D.S.G. (1992) A longitudinal study of primary teachers' perceived competence in, and concerns about, National Curriculum implementation. *Research Papers in Education*, 7(1): 53–78.

Brook, A. and Driver, R. (1984) *The Development of Pupils' Understanding of the Physical Characteristics of Air Across the Age Range 5–16 Years*. Leeds: Children's Learning in Science Project, CSSME, University of Leeds.

Campbell, R.J. and Neill, S.R. St.J. (1994) *Curriculum Reform at Key Stage 1: Teacher Commitment and Policy Failure*. Harlow: Longman, Association of Teachers and Lecturers.

Dearing, R. (1994) *The National Curriculum and its Assessment. Final Report*. London: School Curriculum and Assessment Authority.

DES (1978) *Primary Education in England: A Survey by H.M. Inspectors of Schools*. London: HMSO.

DES (1989a) *Aspects of Primary Education: The Teaching and Learning of Science*. London: HMSO.

DES (1989b) *Science Non-Statutory Guidance*. York: NCC.

DES (1992a) *Designated courses in Mathematics & Science for Primary Teachers: A Report by H.M.I.* Stanmore: DES.

DES (Department of Education and Science) (1992b) *The Implementation of the Curricular Requirements of the Education Reform Act. Science: Key stages 1, 2 and 3. A Report by Her Majesty's Inspectorate 1990–91*. London: HMSO.

Driver, R., Guesne, E. and Tiberghien, A. (eds) (1985) *Children's Ideas in Science*. Milton Keynes: Open University Press.

Driver, R., Squires, A., Rushworth, P. and Wood-Robinson, C. (1994) *Making Sense of Secondary Science – Research into Children's Ideas*. London: Routledge.

Farrow, S. (1992) Science in primary schools: will it ever be a core subject? *The Curriculum Journal*, 3(3): 311–14.

Feasey, R. (1994) The challenge of science, in C. Aubrey (ed.) *The Role of Subject Knowledge in the Early Years of Schooling*. London: Falmer Press.

Kinder, K. and Harland, J. (1991) *The Impact of INSET: The Case of Primary Science*. Slough: NFER.

Leach, J., Driver, R., Scott, P., Wood-Robinson, C. (1992) *Progression in Understanding of Ecological Concepts by Pupils Aged 5 to 16*. Leeds: Children's Learning in Science Research Group, CSSME, University of Leeds.

Nuffield Junior Science Project (1967) Glasgow: Collins.

Nuffield Primary Science (1993) Glasgow: Collins Educational.

OFSTED (Office for Standards in Education) (1993a) *Science Key Stages 1, 2 and 3. Third Year 1991–92*. London: HMSO.

OFSTED (1993b) *Science Key Stages 1, 2, 3 and 4. Fourth Year 1992–93*. London: HMSO.

OFSTED (1993c) *Curriculum Organisation & Classroom Practice in Primary Schools – A Follow Up Report*. London: Department for Education.

Pollard, A., Broadfoot, P., Croll, P., Osborn, M. and Abbot, D. (1994) *Changing English Primary Schools? The Impact of the Education Reform Act at Key Stage One*. London: Cassell.

Russell, T., Qualter, A., McGuigan, L. and Hughes, A. (1993) *Evaluation of the Implementation of Science in the National Curriculum at Key Stages 1, 2 and 3. Final Report*. Liverpool: Centre for Research in Primary Science and Technology, University of Liverpool.

Schools Council (1972) *Science 5–13 Project: Units for Teachers*. London: Macdonald.

SPACE (Science Processes and Concept Exploration) *Research Reports* (1990–94) Liverpool: Liverpool University Press.

Summers, M. (1992) Improving primary school teachers' understanding of science concepts – theory into practice. *International Journal of Science Education*, 14(1): 25–40.

Wragg, E.C., Bennett, S.N. and Carré, C.G. (1989) Primary teachers and the National Curriculum. *Research Papers in Education*, 4(3): 17–37.

5	# DESIGN AND
	# TECHNOLOGY AND
	# INFORMATION
	# TECHNOLOGY
	Helen Constable

In 1989 a new phrase entered the vocabulary of the primary classroom. Children were heard to say that they were 'doing technology'. This ambiguous phrase is indicative of the confusion which has surrounded the Technology Statutory Order. The original Order consisted of two profile components: Design and Technology and Information Technology. In 1994 the Dearing Review recommended that Information Technology be treated as a separate 'subject'. Design and Technology was conceived of as the exploration of a process, a way of doing and thinking, and Information Technology as a cross-curricular resource for learning. For the purposes of this chapter, Design and Technology and Information Technology will be discussed separately.

DESIGN AND TECHNOLOGY

Implementing the Orders

The processes of designing and making in Design and Technology were familiar to Early Years practitioners who were used to teaching through structured play and art and craft activities. However, the technical language of the 1989 Order alienated Key Stage One teachers. The wording was jargonistic and unfamiliar, and in-service training provision to help them understand the new subject was thin on the ground and, according to HMI (1993), declining fast as LEA Advisory services were axed. There were many new skills and concepts that teachers needed to acquire: to learn about structures and mechanisms; how to identify needs and evaluate; how to use tools and work with resistant materials. None of this had been included in the training of any but the most recently qualified teachers. Most primary teachers felt de-skilled and ill informed.

Primary teachers *are* experienced managers of practical work. They have organizational strategies for managing activities which require a large amount of teacher attention and are adept at juggling their time between working groups. However, the prospect of introducing an activity with which they were not yet comfortable themselves, whilst still managing the rest of the classroom activities, was daunting (HMI 1991a).

Some serving teachers were lucky enough to gain places on courses run by LEAs but many of these courses were skills based and did not pay attention to exploring the underlying process and purpose behind Design and Technology activities. Teachers came away knowing how to make a tipper truck using hydraulic syringes, but with no idea *why* they would ask their pupils to make one, or what activities and thought processes went before and after the task set.

A further issue for primary schools was the expense of consumable resources for Design and Technology. Teachers could no longer be satisfied with supplies of found materials for children's model making. They were expected to offer a variety of media including wood, textiles, graphic materials and food. Schools also had to purchase tools and, perhaps for the first time, primary teachers found themselves using saws, drills and hammers alongside more familiar scissors and masking tape. This presented training needs for a profession largely comprising female teachers who were likely to be unfamiliar with these tools. Many infant teachers still shy away from working with resistant materials, saying that they believe their children are not ready for such experiences. In reality it is more likely to be due to their own understandable lack of confidence.

It was inevitable that introducing a 'new' subject into the curriculum would create difficulties for primary schools. Although HMI reports (1992, 1993) on the teaching of Technology at Key Stages One, Two and Three highlighted the inadequacies in the first year of Design and Technology teaching, they remained sympathetic to primary teachers' struggle pointing out that many teachers found the Design and Technology aspects of the Order unhelpful and difficult to understand. Perhaps because of the inaccessibility of the Order, they reported that it was 'open to differences of interpretation'. By the third year of inspection, HMI noted that 77 per cent of the Design and Technology lessons observed at Key Stage One were 'satisfactory or better', which was a steady improvement on previous years' figures. However, they reported that less time overall was being spent on Design and Technology activities in primary classrooms. They also reported that not all aspects of the Order were being covered and that in 'the great majority of lessons only a limited range of work was taught'.

Teaching and learning Design and Technology

In order to help children make progress in Design and Technology, teachers need to understand the design process; but there are as many definitions of the design process as there are designers. There are cyclical or loop models, detailing stages such as the identification of a problem, exploration of ideas to solve the problem, the realization of one of those ideas and some form of evaluation. An early example is Kimbell's interacting design loop (see Figure 1).

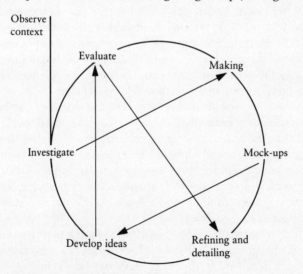

Figure 1 An interacting design loop
Source: *APU (Assessment of Performance Unit)* (1992).

Unfortunately, the very act of separating these stages of the design process transforms what is an essentially holistic process into an apparently linear one, and it is the misconception that designing can be defined as discrete stages in an ordered, sequential process which has underpinned much poor practice. The linear way in which Targets were numbered in the 1989 Order (where the inference was that pupils started by identifying a need and ended up by evaluating the outcome) did not help. The New Order has attempted to get away from a linear framework by subsuming the four Attainment Targets into two global ones, Designing and Making. The holistic *process*, with learners combining a range of strategies at different times as they work through a task, is still the same, however, and if teachers can grasp this theoretical underpinning, they are more likely to be able to plan effective Design and Technology activities for their pupils.

Research published by Anning (1993, 1994) and Constable (1994b) on designing and making activities in the Early Years goes some way to illustrate possibilities in Technology education for young children. Anning studied the features of capability used by children as they tried to solve problems, such as how they visualized solutions and represented their solution in talk, writing or drawing; the ways in which they organized and carried through their emergent ideas; and their abilities to handle materials, tools and equipment in refining the external equivalents of what they saw 'in the mind's eye' into models, plans or systems. Constable's research focused more specifically on children's capabilities in graphicacy in planning and recording ideas; physical/manual skills in making and doing; and in evaluating their own and other peoples' 'products'. Constable's case studies have shown that it is possible to develop children's competence in using tools from an early age, and that they can become adept at handling 'unfamiliar' materials. Makiya and Rogers (1992) argued that the understanding of concepts embedded in designing and making are acquired by children continuously engaging in activities which require them to apply newly acquired skills and 'tinker' with concepts until they are understood. Learning is seen as an iterative process of doing and reflecting on doing, preferably with the support of a more experienced learner.

In all the research the role of an informed adult is seen to enhance children's progress in Design and Technology. However, Anning's work with teachers in the early days of the Technology Order revealed much confusion over what was expected of them. She contrasts the traditionally 'exploratory' nature of the art and craft lesson, which is essentially child-centred, with the direct instruction and careful supervision more likely to be associated with the core subjects. As Design and Technology is an amalgam of the activities of the mind and the hand, which is the best approach to teaching it? A delicate balance needs to be drawn between teaching skills and techniques and providing opportunities for children to find things out for themselves. Early Years teachers are often uncertain about how and when to teach design skills. Many believe that designing and making is about 'discovery' and that they should not interrupt the creative process by teaching children 'how to do it'. However, it *is* necessary to teach skills. Skills are the foundations of Design and Technology Capability and we cannot leave to chance the aquisition of important building blocks. We need to plan to teach the skills of cutting, shaping and joining – didactically if that is the best way – and take time to introduce and demonstrate the processes of hypothesizing, predicting, modifying and evaluating.

In her work on how children approach the original Attainment Target 4, 'Evaluating', Constable (1994a) showed that children in Years 1 and 2 were capable of evaluating the outcome of a design and make activity, be it their own or that of someone else. They could identify the strengths and weaknesses in a design, and comment on its suitability for the job. What they found harder was to identify the criteria by which to make these judgements. This does not seem to come easily to children until the beginning of Key Stage Two. This is where 'scaffolding' by a teacher is so important. Infants need to have criteria suggested to them by the teacher, either directly through examples, or through a carefully structured discussion enabling children to begin to formulate their own criteria.

Constable's work indicated that given criteria, children can and do understand whether a product is 'good' or 'bad', but she asks the question 'Whose criteria should be used?' Teachers need to be alert to values embedded in technological 'advances'. What is good for British industry might be disastrous for a developing country's economy. Constable argues that we must be wary of the values implicit in the assumption that we are making the world a 'better' place to live in through ever advancing technology. Even in the Early Years classroom, teachers need to help children to explore values and differing priorities. It is helpful to think in terms of 'winners and losers'. Who gains from new technology? What are the drawbacks? Thus we begin to sow in children's minds the seeds of how value judgements are made.

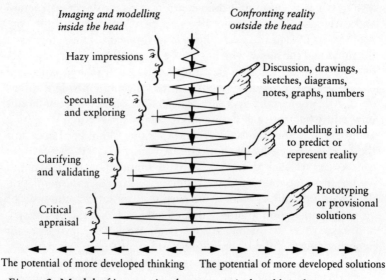

Figure 2 Model of interaction between mind and hand
Source: *APU (Assessment of Performance Unit)* (1992).

Children who have difficulty in expressing themselves on paper
may do well in practical activities. The Assessment of Performance
Unit team (APU 1981) presented a model of Design and Technology
as an iterative process involving the interaction of what goes on in
the head with the practical outcome of those ideas. This is illustrated
in the APU model of the interaction between the mind and the hand
(see Figure 2). It is not necessary to formalize any part of the process
in writing. Pupils can succeed in technology through verbal communication and dexterity of hands. This makes it an ideal vehicle for
learning, whatever the child's ability. However, there is an unfortu-
nate attitude that Design and Technology is intellectually undemanding. There is *much* to occupy the brain when designing and making
– hypothesizing, modifying, predicting, evaluating – and, where
appropriate, recording in written or graphic form.

In the new ethos of market forces and accountability, a major
concern is the way in which what happens in schools is perceived by
outsiders. Teachers may have to work hard to explain to parents
what Design and Technology is about. The tendency is for technology to be seen by visitors in terms of the end product and it may be

difficult to persuade parents that outcomes in Design and Technology are only as important as the processes by which they were achieved.

The following case studies exemplify some effective practice in Key Stage One Design and Technology.

Case study one

Rainbow class is in a large infants school in a semi-industrialized town in the East Midlands. The children mainly come from working-class families with a high proportion of single-parent households. The class teacher, who has been teaching for just under five years, has recently been on a DFE 20-day Technology course.

The running of all practical activities in the school is well managed. There is a coordinator for Design and Technology whose responsibility it is to oversee the whole school policy, provision of resources and maintenance of equipment. Children are encouraged to select resources from a central area. The novelty value of resources for children during their first year of school means they often want to grab everything, but this behaviour is soon converted into thoughtful selection of what to use. Sensitive negotiation with the teacher or a non-teaching adult is often helpful to avoid young children making inappropriate choices or wasting materials.

The school is close to the construction site of a new A1/M1 link road, and has chosen this as a focus for topic work. An education officer from the construction company visited the school and spoke with the class teachers about planning for a site visit. The children were able to watch the road building from a safe distance. The Rainbow class teacher was apprehensive at first about whether the girls in her class would find the visit exciting. However, she observed that any gender bias in the activity was one of her own construction and all her pupils enjoyed the experience.

Having met with key site personnel, the teachers started planning by asking themselves the sort of questions children might ask: 'What's that for? How does that work? Why does that happen?' They divided the questions into broad categories. For example, they listed safety as an area for investigation, including clothing, headgear, shoes, fencing, warning notices and so on. Another area of enquiry arose from a query about where the workmen went to the toilet. They began to look at rest period, catering and workers sleeping arrangements. Plant and machinery was another obvious area of study, although it was noticeable that it was not foremost in their minds.

Back at school, teachers interpreted the topic in the way which they felt best suited the needs of their own class. Rainbow class became interested in the workers' clothing. They listed the sorts of clothing that people on a building site would wear. The discussion moved to the notion of visibility and reflective colours and the children brought in examples of their own reflective clothing.

Case study two

Class Two is a mixed Year 2/3 class in a small rural first school. Many of the children come from local families who have been in the village for generations but there are an increasing number of 'incomers' from more expensive houses. The class teacher, who is also the head, confesses to being apprehensive about his ability to teach Design and Technology.

Class Two also visited the A1/M1 link road construction site, but the pupils' interests were channelled towards the 'hard' technology of the plant and machinery. They made representations of the machinery in a variety of media – construction kits, recycled materials, painting and drawing, clay and modroc. The teacher observed that the children were representing what they remembered on a superficial level, and decided that they would investigate concepts in greater detail before going any further with the project. The children were asked to bring in mechanical toys which showed, for example, how a crane operated or how wheels were joined to an axle. Predictably, this brought an enthusiastic response from the boys, but the majority of the girls felt left out. The teacher endeavoured to involve the girls by asking what else they might find in the classroom to illustrate the key mechanical concepts. They were quick to point out examples such as the wheels on the television trolley. One girl said that the pivoting arm on the class balances was 'a bit like a crane 'cos it goes up and down'. In Design and Technology, it is important to provide a balance of experiences and to pay particular attention to the needs of girls. Even this experienced teacher found himself falling into the trap of steering activities towards 'male' interests.

Assessment

The first non-mandatory Key Stage One Standard Assessment Tasks (SATs) in Technology were offered in 1992. They were taken up by a significant number of teachers who wished to find some way of formalizing hazy impressions of their pupils' Design and Technology Capability. If they achieved nothing else, the SATs produced some excellent class work in Design and Technology and Information Technology. The tasks were carefully structured and clearly described so that even the most hesitant teacher was able to get children working successfully.

However, the mechanisms by which the children's work was assigned a National Curriculum level and the interpretations by teachers of the Statements of Attainment were not reliable. They differed widely between schools and LEAs. One of the four SATs was easier, enabling children who did this task to 'achieve' higher levels. With the threat at the time of published league tables, there was pressure on schools to produce 'good results'. Even teachers who were scrupulously fair had difficulty standardizing their judgements with colleagues in other schools because they were trying to assess an unfamiliar subject. HMI (1993) noted that teachers were uncertain about the standards they should expect and often referred to pupils' experiences and attitudes rather than their technological competence. Research conducted amongst Year 2 teachers in a South London Borough (Constable 1993) indicated that accurate assessment in Design and Technology and Information Technology relied more on the confidence and competence of the teacher than their pupils! Children whose class teachers were secure about Technology were assessed far more accurately, whereas assessment by more hesitant teachers was sometimes done at a superficial level.

We should perhaps question the reliability of the testing *procedure* underpinning the 1992 SATs which required teachers to look at four parts of a holistic process as separate entities, and then tack on a fifth, totally unrelated area (Information Technology Capability) to achieve an aggregate mark for 'Technology'. Thankfully, three years on, the assessment of Design and Technology is to be through Teacher Assessment though teachers may draw on exemplar assessment tasks to assign children to levels. Whilst this relieves Key Stage One teachers of the burden of formal set SATs, it does open up the possibility of teachers electing to assess only those parts of Design and Technology processes which they understand. Moreover, in terms of status, a subject which has to be formally assessed and moderated is still perceived by many as being more important than one which does not.

The Dearing Review

The new Technology Order Programme of Study states that 'Pupils should be taught to develop their design and technology capability through combining their designing and making skills with know-ledge and understanding in order to design and make products' (DFE/Welsh Office 1995a). The Order is lighter in content, easier to understand and purports to be simpler to manage in the classroom. However, it is based on the knowledge and understanding of Design and Technology which has grown out of previous incarnations, and unless teachers have a thorough understanding of the subject, there is the risk that Technology will become a series of superficial one-off 'making' activities, and that the holistic nature of designing and making will be lost.

INFORMATION TECHNOLOGY

Progress in Information Technology

Contemporary society demands Information Technology skills of everyone. Without realizing it we all make use of information systems whenever we go through the supermarket checkout, fill up our petrol tanks or extract money from a hole in the wall. Children are adept at manipulating video recorders, CD players and electronic games. Even the humble washing maching now boasts microchip technology. We are all Information Technology consumers, though children seem to take more readily to new technologies than adults and it is reasonable to assume, therefore, that much of the learning which goes on in school will be through Information Technology (HMI 1991b).

The technology we use in schools today was unimaginable a decade ago. Young children are using the sort of equipment with ease which was the province of professional communicators and data handlers. At Key Stage One they use sophisticated desktop publishing software to present written and graphical work, discover which is the most popular pet using a database, or compose a musical sequence from a pre-set selection of phrases, all by computer. But the introduction of Information Technology has not been without tauma and controversy. From the early days of the BBC and 380z, teachers have had to keep up with rapid advancements in technology. Though some schools are fortunate enough to have the time, finances and expertise to explore the world of scanners, colour printing and CD-ROM, the reality for most primaries is one of struggling with underfunding and lack of time to maintain basic Information Technology provision.

Schools which have not had a systematic policy for replacement of equipment are now finding themselves with large numbers of outdated computers. Even generously resourced schools are hard pressed to provide more than one computer per class. Schools may have old BBCs and newer Acorns or similar machines. Each computer should be used for what it does best: the BBC is excellent for control work whereas newer machines are good for graphics and text manipulation. There might also be a programmable robot in school – PiP or Roamer, for example. It is important to recognize that Information Technology is not *just* computers. Each class is likely to have access to a tape recorder, and possibly a camera or video recorder, 'information technology' which can be used to enhance Information Technology Capability in different ways.

State of the art equipment is not necessary to produce worthwhile learning opportunities. It is not so much a question of how up to date the equipment is, but of knowing how to use it in a meaningful way. For example, writing a story on a piece of paper and then copying it using the computer is not good practice. Using the computer to help draft, redraft, edit and spell-check work is a far better use of a word processor. Similarly, exploring patterns and shapes in art and design by fast replication and repetition on the screen is a lot less laborious than drawing by hand.

Knowing which software is appropriate for Early Years is not always easy. Using a limited range of software *well* rather than giving the children access to lots of programs which they will not fully exploit, is the best strategy. A well-balanced Key Stage One package will include a word processor, a database, a graphics program, modelling software and possibly some music software. A bank of ready made images, known as Clip Art, is also valuable for enhancing children's work and providing stimulus material. With these resources, infant teachers can cover the Information Technology Programme of Study for Key Stage One.

With a typical ratio of one computer to thirty children, teachers have to consider how best to maximize their use. One large, nine-class infant school allocates its computers to working bays. There are three classes to a bay and one computer is placed centrally in each area. Children from each class use the computer on an allocated day, which means that children can use the computer only once every three days. Given an average class size of twenty-three, children get little time to develop their Information Technology skills. In a small rural primary school, all the Key Stage One children are in one class. They have their own computer to which they have access all day every day. On the surface it would appear that these two classes differ greatly in the amount of access pupils have to computers but, surprisingly, the teacher in the small rural school estimates that her pupils only use the computer on average about twice a week. Even one computer per class may not be adequate.

Information Technology is a great motivator (Underwood and Underwood 1990). Children who have difficulty in concentrating in 'ordinary' classroom activities will sit for a long time grappling with an adventure simulation. Why is this? Explanations offered are that children are motivated because working on a computer takes them along at their own pace; it does not look despairingly at them when they fail, and they can try the same exercise time and time again without having to report to an authority figure. It can also challenge the cognitive abilities of gifted children and provide opportunities for individualized programmes of study designed to stretch them.

Whilst acknowledging some good practice in Early Years Information Technology, HMI reports (1992, 1993) highlighted the erratic ways in which Information Technology resources were sometimes managed and a bias towards coverage of certain elements of the Statutory Order. Communicating Information, for example, was covered through the use of word processors, but communication using sound and pictures was less well exploited. Pupils got little experience of Handling Information. This can be done through a simple database or on a CD-ROM. Few Key Stage One classes have access to CD-ROMs yet, but a database program can be acquired quite cheaply and can open up huge areas of learning.

Case study three

A Year 1 class in a large first and middle school has twenty-eight full-time pupils. There is a hearing unit attached to the school and two pupils from the unit join the class for part of the day. The teacher is nearing retirement and has taught in Early Years all her life. She is keen to embrace new ideas, but admits that she is terrified by Information Technology. The Information Technology coordinator in the school has set up each class with some basic software according to their individual needs and interests. The Year One class has a BBC Master running a word processor called Folio, and an A4000S running Talking Pendown, Compose World, My World and Pictogram. They have a Roamer, tape recorder and concept keyboard. The teacher can save work onto disc and take it to the communal colour printer if she wants to print off work in colour. Otherwise she uses a black and white inkjet printer attached to the A4000S, or a dot matrix printer with the BBC machine.

This term's topic was 'People who help us'. The children had a visit from the school nurse, lollipop lady and community policeman. With the help of a non-teaching adult, they all found the words and pictures for these three people on a pre-prepared concept keyboard overlay and got the words to appear on the screen. The words were printed in a large font and stuck under photographs of the visitors taken by some of the children with the school camera. Others 'interviewed' the visitors using the class tape recorder. They decided in advance what questions they would ask and took it in turns to hold the microphone. They played back the answers to the non-teaching adult who typed some of the sentences into the talking word processor. The speech facility allowed the pupils to listen to what was being written as it appeared on the screen. The children with hearing impairments were able to hear the words through their hearing aids.

Another group worked out how to cross the road outside school using the programmable robot. Their task was to programme Roamer to go forward, turn right and cross over a 'zebra crossing' which had been chalked onto the corridor floor. They did preparatory work as part of a whole class lesson in the hall, where children guided other 'robot' children whilst the teacher introduced the words 'left' 'right' 'forward' and 'backward'.

The exemplar shows how the most reticent teacher, with support, can offer relevant Information Technology experiences to Key Stage One pupils.

Assessment

Assessment of Information Technology Capability can be a logistical nightmare with thirty children and only one machine. Experience of the non-mandatory Standard Assessment Tasks in 1992 highlighted this predicament but encouraged some excellent Information Technology practice in schools which took on the challenge.

Assessment of Information Technology is only successful within a carefully planned and closely focused activity, for which learning objectives have been identified, and the task carefully structured to allow capability to be demonstrated. But how much day-to-day Information Technology activity is like this? The problem lies with the nature of the beast – computers misbehave, programs do not load, printers will not work and children stray off task and these niggling problems nibble away at teachers' well-intentioned plans.

Should Information Technology Capability be the subject of assessment in the first place? It is a skill not a subject, a tool for learning rather than a topic to be explored. We do not teach, learn or assess other skills in isolation, but through the medium of a subject or theme. Similarly, Information Technology skills are best acquired, used and assessed through the medium of other curriculum areas, so we are not only assessing the child's Information Technology Capability (the ability to learn through Information Technology) but also the understanding of a given subject through the medium of Information Technology (learning with Information Technology).

The Dearing Review

The Dearing Review has resulted in a simplification of the Information Technology Order and removed many specific references to Information Technology in other subject Orders. For Information Technology Capability the expected achievements of most children at the end of Key Stage One is defined as: 'Pupils use IT to help them generate and communicate ideas in different forms, such as text, tables, pictures and sound. With some support, they retrieve and store work. They use IT to sort and classify information and to present their findings. Pupils control devices purposefully and describe the effects of their actions. They use IT-based models or simulations to investigate options as they explore aspects of real and imaginary situations' (DFE/Welsh Office, 1995b). Information Technology is defined as a basic skill in the Dearing Review.

Teachers have had five years in which to build up their confidence in using Information Technology and there *is* evidence of good practice (HMI 1993; NCET 1994). However, there is still a need for a pyramid of advice and support for class teachers from a coordinator, headteacher, advisers and in-service providers. Moreover, it is acknowledged that primary classrooms are chronically under-resourced in Information Technology.

CONCLUSION

The Dearing recommendations do away with the 1988 Act marriage of convenience of Design and Technology and Information Technology under the Technology banner. We now have two separate curriculum areas with their own identities and their own terms of reference. We must no longer think of 'Technology' as a single curriculum area, rather a curriculum area (D&T) and a learning resource (IT) through which we can teach all other subjects, including Design and Technology.

REFERENCES

Anning, A.J.E. (1993) Technological Capability in primary classrooms, in J.S. Smith (ed.) *IDATER '93 Conference Publication*. Loughborough: Loughborough University Department of Design and Technology.

Anning, A.J.E. (1994) Technological Capability in the primary classroom. *Education for Capability Research Group, Occasional Paper No. 6*. Leeds: University of Leeds School of Education.

APU (Assessment of Performance Unit) (1981) *Design and Technological Activity: A Framework for Assessment*. London: APU/DES.

APU (Assessment of Performance Unit) (1992) Learning through design and technology, in R. McCormick, P. Murphy and M. Harrison (eds) *Teaching and Learning Technology*. Wokingham: Addison Wesley for The Open University.

Constable, H.J. (1993) A note on the first Technology Assessment Tasks at Key Stage One. *Journal of Technology and Design Education*, 3: 3.

Constable, H.J. (1994a) How do Children Evaluate? *Primary DATA*, 3(3): 18–23.

Constable, H.J. (1994b) A study of aspects of Design and Technology Capability at Key Stages 1 & 2, in J.S. Smith (ed.) *IDATER '94 Conference Publication*. Loughborough: Loughborough University Department of Design and Technology.

DFE/Welsh Office (1995a) *Design and Technology in the National Curriculum*. London: HMSO.

DFE/Welsh Office (1995b) *Information Technology in the National Curriculum*. London: HMSO.

HMI (1991a) *Aspects of Primary Education: The Teaching and Learning of Design and Technology*. London: HMSO.

HMI (1991b) *Aspects of Primary Education: The Teaching and Learning of Information Technology*. London: HMSO.

HMI (1992) *Technology at Key Stages 1, 2 & 3: A Report by HM Inspectorate on the First Year, 1990–91*. London: HMSO.

HMI (1993) *Technology at Key Stages 1, 2 & 3: A Report by HM Inspectorate on the Second Year*. London: HMSO.

Makiya, H. and Rogers, M. (1992) *Design and Technology in the Primary School: Case Studies for Teachers*. London: Routledge.

National Council for Educational Technology (1994) *Information Technology Works*. London: NCET.

Underwood, J. and Underwood, G. (1990) *Computers and Learning*. Oxford: Blackwell.

6

GEOGRAPHY

Patrick Wiegand

The quality of Early Years Geography teaching just before the introduction of the National Curriculum seems to have been disappointing. HMI evidence (DES 1978, 1982) indicates that much of it was superficial and that there was little attention paid to continuity and progression. Map reading, way finding and other geographical skills were not generally taught in any systematic way, if they were taught at all. The situation appears to have improved a little by the late 1980s but even then the inspectors were still reporting that only a quarter of all pupils were found to be achieving satisfactory standards or better in work relating to maps, atlases and globes, and there was an almost total absence of studies at a national or world scale. The share of curriculum time allocated to Geography (in whatever guise) and the level of its resourcing in schools was generally found to be inadequate (HMI 1989). Most of the best work tended to be related to the immediate locality of the school but children learnt little of the wider world beyond their immediate experience.

The HMI surveys reveal much geographical work in the Early Years taking place through the medium of topic or project work. This is not of itself problematic but there are potential weaknesses in the approach. The most significant of these is that the distinctive contributions of the subjects most commonly involved (typically Geography, History and Religious Education), and their conceptual structures, are lost to children. The commitment of many primary teachers to 'children rather than subjects' has, however, been inconsistent. Certain subjects (such as Mathematics and Science) have generally been referred to by name, adequately resourced by structured published materials and undertaken in the morning, whereas others (such as Geography and History) have been sub-sumed within topics, resourced out of cardboard boxes with teacher-made materials and undertaken in the afternoon.

Undoubtedly there was some good geographical work to be found in the Early Years and HMI provided some evidence for it. A survey of visits, for example to ten primary schools selected for their known interest in teaching Geography to 5 to 7-year-olds, reported that the attainment in geographical enquiry, skills and knowledge 'often appeared to match or exceed' that expected by what was then being proposed for the National Curriculum (DES 1990). Yet, the overwhelming situation remained that as described by Alexander, Rose and Woodhead (1992: 7) 'much topic work has been and still is, very undemanding, particularly in history and geography'.

What difference has the National Curriculum made to teaching and learning Geography in the Early Years? From the fairly patchy evidence available we can consider three main sets of influences and examine each in turn. First, it has established the identity of the subject within the curriculum; second, it has stimulated research into young children's understanding of key concepts; and third, it has improved curriculum planning and resourcing.

CURRICULUM IDENTITY AND DEFINITION

It was not surprising that, as the shape of the National Curriculum for Geography began to emerge through the various draft and interim proposals to the final Statutory Orders, many primary teachers found themselves puzzled at the apparent mismatch be-tween what the subject appeared to be and what they might have thought it was. Geography is of course a large and diverse discipline. A wide range of specialists such as economists, mathematicians, sociologists, planners, physicists, cartographers, computer scientists or philosophers, might each call themselves geographers because the central focus of their interests is the concept of place. Not only that, but the way in which geographers have pursued their enquiries has been subject to a number of changes in recent years. Such changes have been referred to as 'revolutions', during each of which the

prevailing methodologies have been rooted in, for example, quanti-
tative techniques or the behavioural sciences. It was not surprising,
therefore, that the diversity of the subject and the speed of change
had not left a clear message for the non-specialist, so that many
primary teachers had little idea of what Geography really was, what
it might include at school level and how it might best be learnt. The
1991 Statutory Orders, with their clear definition of Geography as
skills, knowledge and understanding of places and the three parallel
themes (physical, human and environmental), set out the range and
scope of the subject for the first time for primary schools.

Such a discussion of the character of Geography is significant
precisely because Geography *is* part of the National Curriculum. It
very nearly was not. We now readily accept that the National
Curriculum is composed of 'subjects'. However, at the time there
were persuasive arguments for alternatives such as that based, for
example, on so-called 'areas of experience' (HMI 1985). But even
though it was clear that the prevailing ideology favoured (one cannot
say argued for) a subject-based curriculum it was by no means clear
that geography, considered to have low status, would be included in
the list. The activities of the Geographical Association at this time
were of the utmost importance in defending and securing the place of
the subject. At a critical stage the Secretary of State, Sir Keith Joseph,
was invited to address the Association and officers responded
promptly by publishing an answer to his challenge to justify the
contribution that Geography could make to the curriculum. An
energetic 'shadow' working party published a draft of how the
curriculum might look which was available for the first 'official'
working party when it commenced its discussions. These activities
not only helped establish the subject's position but also clarified its
relationship with other cross-curricular themes such as environmental education, peace education, political education and multi-
cultural education.

When the National Curriculum began to emerge, the collaborative
efforts of many to secure the survival of the subject ensured that there
was a high level of consensus among the Geography education
community about what was appropriate to be taught in school. The
National Curriculum documentation was a milestone in that it was
the first broadly agreed definition of primary Geography. Yet the
entire process had been dominated by specialist geographers rather
than by specialist primary educators (of whom there had been only
one on the working party which drafted the Programmes of Study

and Statements of Attainment). The resultant documents as they emerged therefore tended to be rather technical in tone and were in parts fairly unintelligible to non-specialists. This applied particularly to Geographical Skills which had been given prominence in order to emphasize the subject's distinctiveness but which was the very area where teachers had been shown to be most vulnerable. Some fairly demanding criteria were also set for the study of places – such as the requirement that children should study a locality in an economically developing country.

When, therefore, Early Years non-specialist teachers received the Geography Statutory Orders they were in receipt of the outcome of a political struggle for the subject's survival and status, as well as an attempt to distil from a diverse and rapidly changing discipline a workable definition for schools. Many teachers first read the Orders with apprehension, as is demonstrated by the evidence presented in the report of the monitoring exercise undertaken by the British sub-committee of the Commission for Geography Education of the International Geographical Union (Naish 1992). Nevertheless, despite an inauspicious start and perhaps as a tribute to energetic INSET activity, the first five years appears to have been a time of growing confidence. In part this has been due to an increasing awareness that much familiar material is still appropriate. 'People who help us' *are* Geography! There has also been for many teachers a relief that a framework of basic factual knowledge (such as naming the continents) is required.

SOME GAINS IN CHILDREN'S UNDERSTANDING OF GEOGRAPHY

There are substantial gaps in our understanding of children's learning in Geography. In fact one writer has claimed that we know more about the ecology of baboons than we do about children's use of and relationship to their immediate environment (Hart 1983). The National Curriculum has, however, stimulated research into two principal areas: children's knowledge and understanding of places, and children's use of maps.

Much of the traditional emphasis in the Early Years on the immediate locality of the school appears to have been based on the belief that very young children's learning must be rooted solely in concrete phenomena and their own direct experience. This is not to deny that such direct experience is not a vital part of young children's development but the view does conflict with some of the strongest areas of interest held by young children such as dinosaurs or space which are, in some senses at least, both abstract and remote. The study of distant people and places, therefore, came to be neglected despite the fact that a growing body of evidence suggested that even if children were not in direct contact themselves with other cultures, they were in contact with the prevailing attitudes towards them. Many such attitudes are racist and these are frequently passed to children. Jeffcoate (1977) shows, for example, that a group of nursery children not only used racist language but were able to modify its use according to whether an adult was present or not. Teaching towards positive attitudes needs to begin early and the work of the World Studies and Global Education movements has done much to provide exemplar material for teachers. In this connection, Fountain (1990) provides a helpful collection of suggested collaborative activities suitable for 4 to 7-years-olds designed to enable children to learn to listen to others' point of view, to be tolerant and to talk about and to value their own thoughts, feelings and ideas.

What do very young children know about the wider world? A study of the 'known world' of the nursery attempted to plot all the distant places recalled by name by eighty 3 to 5-year-olds before the introduction of the National Curriculum (Lambert and Wiegand 1990). Using pictures, models, toys and artefacts as well as imaginative play (such as a 'magic carpet' on which children could travel anywhere they could name) to elicit information from the children, a record was kept of all the places mentioned in conversations and spontaneous talk. At this age the typical known world seemed to consist of Spain, France, Africa, America and Australia. By the end of Key Stage One it appeared to have widened to consist now of France, Spain, Greece, Russia, China, India, Australia, America and Africa (Wiegand 1991a). What is known *about* these places and the pictures children might have of them in their minds is more variable but it seems likely that a number of discrete 'environments' begin to emerge as the first building blocks of place awareness. These theme parks of the mind form 'worlds': each one differentiated from the other and associated with typical features. Very early on children develop fairly clear images of, for example, a Spanish beach resort, a jungle, a desert margin landscape and a tropical island. The sources of such images are varied but include television, books, comics, information from members of the family and, increasingly, the children's own travel (Wiegand 1991b). The extent of children's travel experiences has yet to be fully recognized but such experiences as they do have form an important part of the way they respond in school to pictures and stories about distant places. Even a single week on the Costa del Sol provides some basic framework for thinking about homes, clothes, weather and food in distant lands and consequently a starting point for teachers to develop. It is becoming clear that children do in fact have a greater store of travel experience than has hitherto been recognized.

These investigations into children's place knowledge have been fairly small and localized and it is regrettable that the opportunity for monitoring the effect of this radical programme of teaching about specific key places was not taken at a national scale. Nevertheless, similar studies to those above were carried out in 1994 and the results have been encouraging. Children were asked to draw freehand sketch maps of the world and to label or name places they knew. The results reveal firstly that some children possess an extraordinary ability to recall the world map, including details of shape and place names but secondly that there appear to be some distinctive ways in which the information is recorded in map form (Wiegand 1995). The work also points to some helpful strategies that can be used in teaching place knowledge. Many children for example find it difficult to appreciate that places 'nest' inside each other (counties inside countries inside continents) and explicit teaching of this point can be helpful, making use of simple cut out shapes that fit one inside the other. Generalizing the world map into simple outline ovals can also be helpful for children learning the relative locations of the continents as many are overfaced with the complexity of coastlines. It is likely that this sort of simplification in the Early Years will help build a durable mental reference system for places as children develop.

As well as stimulating interest in young children's awareness of the wider world the National Curriculum has helped focus attention on children's ability to use large-scale maps. This is to be welcomed as it now seems clear that some of the complex skills involved in using maps can be undertaken by children earlier than has been generally recognized, especially if the context in which the tasks are presented is meaningful. Children will, in free play, use blocks to represent houses and other buildings and assemble these into representations of large scale environments such as villages and parts of a town. As a result of experiences like this they may come to spontaneously understand the formal conventions of maps. For example, when shown a map representing a possible urban environment and consisting of standard symbols representing houses, roads, churches, etc., a group of 4 to 6-year-olds appeared to be able to name the symbols even though they had no prior training and the map had no key (Blades and Spencer 1987).

Children aged 3 to 5 can use simple maps to find objects in a room (Bluestein and Acredolo 1979) and to follow a route (Blades and Spencer 1986a) but both these studies highlight potential difficulties that some children may have and perhaps why for some time it was widely believed that such skills were beyond the scope of many young children. In these two examples the task is readily undertaken by young children providing that the map is correctly oriented at the outset. It is this that is the stumbling block for many, not the task itself. Similarly very young children are usually able to use coordinates on maps but are more consistently accurate if the grid is identified by colours and/or shapes than by letters and numbers (Blades and Spencer 1986b).

CURRICULUM PLANNING AND RESOURCES

Although the National Curriculum is structured around subjects, most geographical work at Key Stage One is still (quite appropriately) delivered through tried and tested topics such as Myself, Shops, Houses, Food, Our School, Where We Live and People Who Help Us. Perhaps one of the most significant outcomes of the first five years of the National Curriculum is that these popular topics most often appear now as part of a school curriculum policy framework to ensure continuity, progression and balanced coverage for children. In many cases the topics themselves have been derived from an appraisal of what the locality of the school can offer in the way of geographical potential for children's learning. This might typically have consisted of the identification of safe places within easy walking of the school where geographical studies can be undertaken, such as viewpoints, landform features, places of work, services, environmental improvements, etc.

Geography is a strongly resource-based subject. Children need access to evidence about places – in the form of photographs, videotape, maps, artefacts, travellers' tales, stories, music, and even preparing food and dressing up. Whilst teachers have always seen it as part of their professional skill to create materials for use in the classroom, new curriculum demands often require inputs from specialists. In 1989 most published geography resources were in the form of series of text books. By 1994 all the major publishers had comprehensive schemes for primary Geography in more imaginative formats, including teacher support materials, 'big book' picture and atlas resources, photo packs, individual children's readers and photocopiable masters. However, it has been the requirement that children study a locality in another part of the world that compares in scale with their own home area that has stimulated the most exciting resource developments of the National Curriculum. In particular the voluntary aid agencies have used their local knowledge to create photo packs that form the basis for detailed study of distant places, especially in economically developing countries. One of the earliest was the best-selling *Chembakolli* – featuring a village in India and published by Action Aid. Good though many of these materials are, they are really no substitute for what skilled teachers often do best – creating their own materials for use with children whose specific needs they have in mind. It is to be hoped, therefore, that whilst published materials will probably need to fill the gap for localities that are inaccessible to most of us, they will serve as exemplars for resource collections based on teachers' own travel. Good guidance on what sorts of resources to collect and how to go about it is provided in Hughes and Marsden (1994).

The demands of the National Curriculum have also led to the exploitation of story as a resource for learning about places. The popular stories by Jill Tomlinson, for example, dealing with young animals growing up, are in many ways geographical stories. Otto is a penguin chick who lives in the Antarctic (*Penguin's Progress*, Methuen 1975, Magnet 1979) and rapidly learns about survival and climate. The stories by Ruskin Bond about India are similarly rich in local colour and can be used as the starting points for finding out about distant places (*Earthquake*, Walker Books 1989 or *Flames in the Forest*, Young Puffin 1988). Many children's books also contain maps and these can be used to develop map skills as well as extend children's imagination. Good examples include recent stories such as *Summer in Small Street* (Geraldine Kaye, Mammoth 1990), *The Last Bus* (William Mayne, Red Fox 1990) as well as old favourites such as *Milly Molly Mandy* (Joyce Lankester Brisley, George G. Harrap and Co. Ltd 1948) and *Winnie the Pooh* (A.A. Milne, Methuen 1926).

CONCLUSION

The National Curriculum has been good news for Geography. It has a more secure place within the curriculum than it might have had. Case studies show encouraging collaborative work between colleagues in individual schools and a more rationally balanced curriculum agreed by staff. Curriculum documentation has improved and the identification of members of staff with particular responsibility for Geography has ensured more rational use of INSET time, particularly through the successful Grants for Education Support and Training (GEST) funded 20-day courses. Many more primary teachers are seizing opportunities for developing specialist skills. The Geographical Association's journal *Primary Geographer* may be taken as a measure of the growth of interest in Geography. The journal was first published in spring 1989. By November the circulation was 1350 and 5 years later has risen to 5402. Similarly, the Association's annual conference included for the first time in 1989 a 'Primary Day' at which attendance had doubled to 600 by 1993.

Geography is now a statutory entitlement for every child in the Early Years. For the first time teachers are able to see in detail the progression of geographical understanding from (for example) a five-year-old who is learning to 'follow directions' to a sixteen-year-old who is learning to 'evaluate the effectiveness of a composite thematic map as a geographical information system'. It is true that there were some weaknesses with the form of the 1991 Statutory Orders and many teachers have welcomed the slimmer post-Dearing framework. Yet perhaps what will in future be seen as an interim stage in the development of the National Curriculum overall will be viewed as the golden age of Geography in primary schools. It would be ironic if the greater discretion likely to be allowed in curriculum planning prompted a return to less rigour and a dilution of the distinctive contribution geography can make to young children's early learning.

REFERENCES

Alexander, R., Rose, J. and Woodhead, C. (1992) *Curriculum Organisation and Classroom Practice in Primary Schools: A Discussion Paper.* London: DES.

Blades, M. and Spencer, C. (1986a) Map use in the environment and educating children to use maps. *Environmental Education and Information*, 5: 187–204.

Blades, M. and Spencer, C. (1986b) On the starting grid. *Child Education*, December: 23–5.

Blades, M. and Spencer, C. (1987) Young children's recognition of environmental features from aerial photographs and maps. *Environmental Education and Information*, 6: 189–98.

Bluestein, N. and Acredolo, L. (1979) Developmental changes in map reading skills. *Child Development*, 50: 691–7.

DES (1978) *Primary Education in England: A Survey by HM Inspectors of Schools*. London: HMSO.

DES (1982) *Education 5 to 9: An Illustrative Survey of 80 First Schools in England*. London: HMSO.

DES (1990) *Geography in the Early Years: A Report by HMI*. London: HMSO.

Fountain, S. (1990) *Leaning Together: Global Education 4–7*. Cheltenham: Stanley Thorne (Publishers) Co. Ltd.

Hart, R. (1983) Wildlands for children. *Bulletin of Environmental Education*, 141: 5.

HMI (1985) *Curriculum 5–16*. London: HMSO for the Department of Education and Science.

HMI (1989) *Aspects of Primary Education: The Teaching and Learning of History and Geography*. London: HMSO for the Department of Education and Science.

Hughes, J. and Marsden, W. (1994) Resourcing primary geography: bringing the world into the classroom, in Marsden, W. and Hughes, J. (eds) *Primary School Geography*. London: David Fulton Publishers.

Jeffcoate, R. (1977) Children's racial ideas and feelings. *English in Education*, 11: 1.

Lambert, S. and Wiegand, P. (1990) The beginnings of international understanding. *The New Era in Education*, 71: 90–3.

Naish, M. (ed.) (1992) *Primary Schools, Geography and the National Curriculum in England: Monitoring the Implementation of Geography in the National Curriculum*. Sheffield: The Geographical Association.

Wiegand, P. (1991a) The known world of the primary school. *Geography*, 76: 143–9.

Wiegand, P. (1991b) Does travel broaden the mind? *Education 3–13*, 19: 54–8.

Wiegand, P. (1995) Children's free recall of sketch maps of the world. *International Research in Geographical and Environmental Education*, 4(1): 19–28.

7

HISTORY

Elizabeth Wood

Now, what I want is Facts. Teach these boys and girls nothing but Facts. Facts alone are what is wanted in life. Plant nothing else, and root out everything else. You can only form the minds of reasoning animals upon Facts; nothing else will ever be of any service to them.

(Thomas Gradgrind in *Hard Times* by Charles Dickens 1854)

Dickens' quotation came to characterize the sometimes heated debates surrounding the design and implementation of National Curriculum History. It also highlights three fundamental issues which teachers have had to confront during the last five years in their efforts to translate the statutory Order into a workable curriculum. First, teachers needed clear understanding of the nature of History not only in relation to the prescribed content, but also the concepts, skills and methods of enquiry which characterize the discipline. Second, teachers needed information about the development of children's understanding in History not just in terms of how they absorb facts, but how they learn to think, question, investigate and act as historians do. Third, teachers needed knowledge about appropriate methods of teaching and assessment strategies to plan for relevance, progression and continuity in the History curriculum.

This chapter will explore each of these issues with the intention of redressing some misconceptions about the nature of History and its place in the Early Years curriculum. It will examine some of the problems which teachers have encountered in their efforts to incorporate the statutory Order into worthwhile learning experiences. The final section will outline areas of development based on examples of research and practice.

THE NATURE OF HISTORY

History cannot be defined simply in terms of finding out about the past. Like all other disciplines, History is characterized by key concepts, skills, methods and tests for truth and validity. Cooper has outlined a broad definition which takes account of the breadth and complexity of the discipline:

> It is the questions historians ask and the ways they answer them that distinguish history as a discipline. History is concerned with the causes and effects of change over time; with the ways in which, and the reasons why, societies in the past were different from ours and what caused them to change. Historians investigate the past by investigating traces of the past, the evidence. They interpret evidence through a process of deductive reasoning, but evidence is often incomplete . . . and more than one interpretation may be defensible. Producing a range of valid interpretations involves thinking which we call 'historical imagination'. A wide, perceptive range of valid interpretations may eventually lead to an understanding of why people in the past may have thought and felt as they did.
>
> (1992: 6)

On the basis of this definition, History might be considered as beyond the understanding and experience of children in the Early Years of school. However, Marwick's view (1970) that understanding the past is a basic human need and instinct, applies just as much to children as adults. Children are spontaneously connected to their own past through their families, their environment, the media and their shared cultural heritage.

History, like Geography, did not enjoy a secure place in the Early Years curriculum prior to the introduction of the National Curriculum. Evidence from HMI (DES 1989a) raised several concerns about History in the primary school including a lack of clear aims, inappropriate methods of teaching, and inconsistent approaches to planning and assessment. Only one in five infant schools or departments was judged to be satisfactory or better. Reasons for the 'very disappointing standards' included lack of curriculum leadership and clearly defined curriculum policy, limitations in teachers' subject knowledge and perceived weakness in topic-based or integrated approaches to curriculum design and delivery. In view of its low status, many teachers and historians welcomed its inclusion as a foundation subject across all four key stages.

NATIONAL CURRICULUM HISTORY

The nature and content of History were conceptualized differently by academic historians, educationists and politicians. Consequently the statutory Order was disputed energetically throughout the design and implementation stages (Little 1990). Most of this debate focused on Key Stages Two to Four with relatively little reference to Key Stage One. As with other subjects, primary teachers were under-represented on the working group. The group was to some extent 'dancing in the dark' because of the lack of detailed knowledge on the development of children's understanding in History, but this was only one of several problems to emerge as History was introduced into the primary curriculum.

The Programmes of Study for Key Stage One were not unduly prescriptive. They encompassed a dual focus on knowledge and understanding with the development of skills in historical enquiry and communication. This raised questions about the amount of subject knowledge required by teachers to underpin their teaching and how that knowledge should be represented to young children. As with other subjects, the statements of attainment implied a linear, hierarchical model of progression based on the accretion of knowledge. Some of the statements were not clearly defined and it was doubted whether the ten level descriptors accurately reflected qualitative changes in children's historical thinking. As Harnett noted, 'Specifying the levels of attainment applicable to each Key Stage is problematic; teachers who strictly adhere to the levels specified for the age of their children might underestimate children's abilities and lower their expectations of children's achievements' (1993: 138).

Initially, at least, the introduction of History seemed to raise more problems than it solved. A common view expressed about the Order was that Key Stage One had been kept deliberately simple.

However, this belied a misconception about teaching and learning in the Early Years. What may seem simple to an academic historian is immensely complex to a young child.

By the time History was introduced at Key Stage One in 1991, problems of curriculum overload were already emerging. A report by HMI noted that there was insufficient time for adequate planning, preparation and liaison with curriculum coordinators, as well as for observation, record keeping and assessment (DES 1989b). These issues were recurrent themes in reports which tracked the implementation of the National Curriculum. A study by Evans *et al.* (1994) found that teachers were concentrating time on the core subjects with an average of 4.6 hours per week devoted to the foundation subjects. In their view, this was barely sufficient to ensure a broad and balanced curriculum, let alone 'doing justice to subjects such as art, P.E., technology, history and geography which are practical, time-consuming activities at this stage' (ibid.: 15).

THE DEVELOPMENT OF CHILDREN'S UNDERSTANDING IN HISTORY

Curriculum development was initially constrained by an inadequate research and knowledge base in teaching and learning History, particularly in the Early Years. Knight *et al.* (1991) believed that because of this, a mismatch between children's learning capability and the curriculum was inevitable. Little (1990: 320) argued that at primary level, History was an unintended victim of the spread of Piagetian ideas. Piaget's work on time, language and logico-deductive reasoning offered deficit views of the potential for developing historical understanding in young children. History was not seen as relevant or appropriate for an Early Years curriculum. However, engaging with History is not dependent on a precise understanding of measured time and chronology. There is research evidence that young children do acquire frameworks for the development of temporal understanding, however imprecise these may seem at the outset. Reviews of research (Willig 1990; Cooper 1992; Knight 1993) reveal that many studies have challenged Piaget's ideas.

Recent studies which have examined development and progression in children's historical understanding have focused on the whole primary age range (Cooper 1992; Harnett 1993; Smith and

Holden 1994) and have revealed some interesting commonalities. The development of children's understanding of time and historical concepts is gradual and depends on three interacting elements. First, it is important to recognize the value of children's experiences both in and out of school. In each of these studies children utilized their existing knowledge and conceptual frameworks to assist explanation, analysis and enquiry. Second, successful learning depends on relevant, meaningful contexts which utilize this knowledge and provide appropriate challenges to children's thinking. Third, successful teaching depends on the teacher's knowledge and their ability to draw upon a wide repertoire of teaching strategies and resources.

These three elements are in tune with Vygotskian theories which emphasize the importance of the social and cultural contexts of teaching and learning and the role of the teacher (Meadows 1993). Vygotsky defined a range of 'psychological tools' which assist in the learning process. These can be described as knowledge, skills, processes and sense-making capacities. History represents a distinctive way of thinking and learning and can, therefore, be seen as important in helping children to make sense of the world and create meaning.

Adults need to scaffold children's learning to introduce them to distinctive features of the discipline. For example, as part of a school's centenary celebrations, a role play area was designed by teachers (to be used by infants and juniors) to include a modern and Victorian kitchen. The teachers used a range of artefacts including a dolly tub, a postle, washboard and mangle. They wanted the children to know what these artefacts were called, to understand how they were used, how they compared to modern technology and what they revealed about the lives of people who used them. The children's role play was enriched by this knowledge, resulting in complex sequences of play in which they used their skills and understanding to create stories, roles and characters with evidence of disciplined historical imagination, particularly from Year 2 and above.

TEACHING HISTORY

One of the challenges for teachers has been to provide educational experiences in the classroom which utilize methodological and conceptual rigour in History but at the same time build on children's existing frameworks of skills and concepts. This has raised questions about subject-based approaches to planning, teachers' subject matter knowledge and effective teaching strategies.

Early Years teachers have espoused integrated approaches to planning active, discovery-based learning, and first-hand experience as basic principles. The introduction of the National Curriculum with its subject-based approach seemed to undermine these principles and established practices. One teacher's comment at an in-service course in 1991 was unequivocal, 'History. Absolute rubbish. It's got nothing to do with my children. I'm just not going to teach it'. Such a response was understandable in the face of perpetual curriculum change as well as content overload. However, entrenchment has given way to a more thoughtful consideration of some of these problems and the debate about subject matter knowledge increasingly indicates its importance to teaching and learning in the Early Years (Aubrey 1994).

Subject matter knowledge is a complex issue. It does not simply imply having enough factual or content knowledge to keep one step ahead of the children. Teachers need knowledge about the structure and content of a discipline in order to understand fully its distinctive characteristics. Subject matter knowledge must also be related to their pedagogical knowledge so that it can be represented to young children in relevant, appropriate ways and can be adapted to their understandings. This is particularly important for Early Years practitioners. Giving more status to subject matter and pedagogical knowledge does not imply a fragmented approach to the curriculum, nor does it threaten child-centredness or denigrate active learning and enquiry-based methods. On the contrary, it can help teachers to plan more effectively for integration, with greater understanding of meaningful relationships between curriculum areas as well as their distinctive characteristics. For example, the concept of change means different things to a historian, a geographer and a scientist.

The move to long-term planning has created problems for teachers. One teacher described a five-year rolling programme of topics to be covered across Key Stages One and Two to facilitate progression and prevent repetition. This has emerged as a common whole-school strategy, with year groups taking a different subject focus for each term's planning, to ensure breadth and balance. Such a model can actually unbalance the curriculum in relation to children's patterns of learning. For example, a PGCE student placed in a mixed Year 2/3 class was asked to 'do' the Romans. However, she was unable to plan any related activities in Art, such as designing mosaics or making replica artefacts from clay, because the children had 'done' their Art project the previous term and the Art specialist had moved onto another class. Such inflexible long-term planning models could force teachers into resource pack-dependency and endless worksheets to teach History, ignoring the potential for valuable links across subject areas which genuinely extend aspects of historical thinking such as empathy, historical imagination and storying.

Another teacher described a different approach. Within a broad topic, the theme changed every fortnight in order to cover National Curriculum prescribed content. Within half a term on Our Environment, children in a mixed age class (aged 4 to 6 years) had 'covered' our village, our school, farming, the seaside and the countryside. This 'breathless romp' left little time for developing historical thinking.

Clearly a workable consensus on planning which meets the needs of children across the primary age range is still evolving. On the positive side, the majority of teachers I have worked with have maintained some degree of integration in their planning. This is shown by their use of artefacts. For example – bed warmers, irons and washing implements have been used for Science (Hot and Cold); candles and lanterns for Science (Light); old farming implements for Geography (Food and Farming); tools and utensils for Design and Technology. Using such strategies, many teachers have risen creatively to the challenges presented to them by the statutory History Order.

From initial defensiveness and some entrenchment, Early Years practitioners have begun to reconceptualize their practice in ways which enable them to articulate the immense complexity of teaching young children. They are accepting the constraints on their personal knowledge bases. Adults modelling 'not knowing' and the processes of finding out can be powerful motivators for young children. In evaluating historical evidence, children also have to tolerate uncertainty and recognize the validity of a range of possible explanations.

Nevertheless, the quality of teaching and learning which the National Curriculum demands cannot be delivered without additional professional support and resources. The quick-fix, tips for teacher approach to in-service courses, which accompanied the introduction of the History Order, provided some guidance on activities, but did not always deepen teachers' understandings of the subject or provide a secure foundation for future development.

Discussions with teachers have revealed the unevenness of in-service support in History ranging from none, to one hour's school-based in-service, to modular courses at local higher education institutions. Other concerns which teachers have expressed consistently include the impact on the curriculum for the under fives in both reception and nursery classes, the availability of resources to support learning in History, and the variable quality of published schemes.

WAYS FORWARD

If we refer back to Cooper's definition of History, we must ask at what level are young children capable of engaging with History? Can they understand concepts of change, cause and effect? Can they investigate and interpret evidence and produce a range of valid interpretations? Can they develop a well-informed historical imagination? The following section outlines some examples drawn from action research projects which address these questions. The projects provide insights into ways in which some teachers are moving beyond coping strategies, to developing their practice through enhanced understanding of the nature of History and children's learning in History.

A research project based at Exeter University has started to examine the development of children's understanding in History, focusing on 4 to 11-year-olds (Smith and Holden 1994). The project is based on children's investigation of Victorian artefacts. These were chosen to provide a stimulus to authentic historical investigation and to show evidence of technological change. Where possible, modern equivalents were provided to enable children to compare and contrast the artefacts, make informed deductions about the past and present, and speculate about the everyday lives of people who used them. The teaching approaches and activities can be differentiated according to age, abilities and prior experiences of the children.

Several interesting features have emerged from the project. First, there has been a high level of interest and engagement in the investigations from children of all ages and abilities. Even with unfamiliar objects such as a button hook and sack-grabber, the children have enjoyed guessing and finding out. With the younger children, guesses were sometimes wild, but as teachers interacted appropriately to draw their attention to significant features of an artefact, they began to develop their observational skills and refine their hypotheses.

Early Years teachers are frequently exhorted to begin with the known and move to the unfamiliar. The difficulty with such an approach is that we do not know for sure what is known or unfamiliar and it can become a recipe for benign, unchallenging activities. Providing authentic, challenging contexts for developing historical thinking has demonstrated how children make connections between school-based activities and their informally acquired knowledge outside school. For example, two 4-year-olds knew how a flat iron was heated, one because she had seen it in the film of Cinderella, another because she had seen it on a television programme at home.

From the initial stimulus, further activities were planned using the local environment, visits to historical sites, the museum and library services, displays of artefacts from the children's homes, oral history and developing role play areas with a Victorian theme.

The initial stage of the research project has begun to identify patterns in the development of children's understanding in History. These will be investigated further in the second stage along with implications for teaching and assessment. Findings from the project have also served the purpose of informing Early Years practitioners on in-service courses. The next section reports a study carried out by a teacher as a result of attendance on a modular course at Exeter University.

USING ARTEFACTS

The study was carried out by an experienced Early Years teacher with a mixed age class (aged 4 to 7 years) in a small rural school in Devon. Her aim was to investigate what could be expected of the children in investigating evidence and developing a sense of time. The initial stimulus came from a child who had dug up two pottery jars in a field. Other artefacts were unearthed by the teacher from a hedge bottom and the remains of a barn. They included a coronation mug, a glass bottle, assorted pottery fragments and an old shoe with a crystal glass bead inside. The investigation was guided by a framework of key questions (Smith and Holden 1994).

The findings indicated that children are capable of acting as young historians and thinking historically in ways which are compatible

with Cooper's definition. The children used logic, reasoning, creativity, imagination and a willingness to take risks with their
hypotheses. This is exemplified by a child's description of one of the
jars he found in the field:

> I found the fat one in the football field in the hedge and I saw
> the top peeping out . . . and there was all soil inside. I thought
> I'd just found an ornament but it wasn't. I thought it might
> have diamonds underneath and then I'd be rich but there
> wasn't. I don't think it's old because all the pieces are there. It
> might be a cup from a long time ago without handles but from
> 1,000 years ago it would have been in pieces. The bottom's
> hard and the side the paint (glaze) has come off a bit and it's a
> bit lumpy. It might have been made out of clay and it might
> have been fired . . . I've seen it on the telly a man making pots
> . . . It's got writing on it. I don't know how they did those
> words. They might have done it and scratched the words out
> and then fired it . . . It wouldn't have been very valuable to
> them or they wouldn't have thrown it out because it wasn't
> broken.

The range of the children's existing knowledge surprised the
teacher. They drew on previous experiences, family stories and
reminiscences. They tolerated not knowing for sure, and were
prepared to consider other points of view as having equal validity.
The investigation also inspired some creative storying based on the
crystal bead in the old shoe, but with evidence of disciplined
historical imagination. The study demonstrated how children's
potential can be developed through authentic historical activities
compatible with child-centred, active learning and enquiry-based
approaches to the curriculum.

THE FUTURE OF HISTORY

This chapter has outlined the problems which teachers have faced
during the last five years, and highlighted new areas of research.
History has been retained at Key Stage One in the Dearing Review
but its place may not be entirely secure. Comments from teachers
have indicated concerns about the increased emphasis on the core
subjects but whether this will be at the expense of History or other
foundation subjects remains to be seen. Research into young

children's learning in History is developing and should provide support in refining teachers' knowledge about progression in historical understanding. However, teachers will only gain access to this knowledge if there are courses provided which address the interdependence of subject matter knowledge and pedagogical knowledge, and enable teachers to think critically and reflectively about their own changing practice.

ACKNOWLEDGEMENT

With thanks to Janet Walker of Hennock Primary School for permission to use extracts from her research.

REFERENCES

Aubrey, C. (ed.) (1994) *The Role of Subject Knowledge in the Early Years of School*. London: Falmer Press.
Cooper, H. (1992) *The Teaching of History*. London: David Fulton.
DES (1989a) *The Teaching and Learning of History and Geography*. London: HMSO.
DES (1989b) *The Implementation of the National Curriculum in Primary Schools*. London: HMSO.
Evans, L., Packwood, A., Neill, S.R. St.J. and Campbell, R.J. (1994) *The Meaning of Infant Teachers' Work*. London: Routledge.
Harnett, P. (1993) Identifying progression in children's understanding: the use of visual materials to assess primary school children's learning in history. *Cambridge Journal of Education*, 23(2), entire article.
Knight, P.T. (1993) *Primary History, Primary Geography*. London: David Fulton.
Knight, P.T., Farmer, A. and Hewitt, J. (1991) Implementation and change in the National Curriculum: History in the 1990s, *Education 3–13*, 19(2), entire article.
Little, V. (1990) A National Curriculum in History: a very contentious issue, *British Journal of Educational Studies*. XXXVIII(4), entire article.
Marwick, A. (1970) *The Nature of History*. London: Macmillan.
Meadows, S. (1993) *The Child As Thinker*. London: Routledge.
Smith, E.A. and Holden, C. (1994) I thought it was for picking bones out of soup . . . using artefacts in primary school. *Teaching History*, 76(June), entire article.
Willig, C.J. (1990) *Children's Concepts and the Primary Curriculum*. London: Paul Chapman Publishing.

8

ART

Angela Anning

IDEOLOGIES

Primary teachers have inherited a diversity of traditions and ideologies in the teaching of Art to young children. In Elementary Schools Art was seen as servicing the development of 'Skill of Hand and Eye' for a useful and productive industrial workforce. Art lessons consisted of routine exercises in learning how to draw 3D shapes, copying pictures chalked up on the blackboard by the teacher or from books, or directed exercises in colour identification and patterning (Tomlinson 1947).

In the 1930s Frank Cizek's pioneering work on Child Art having integrity in its own right, rather than 'deficit' adult art, was interpreted and disseminated in the United Kingdom by Marion Richardson. She recommended simple, vivid materials – powder paints, thick brushes and so on – and the need for teachers not to impose adult techniques and standards on children. Richardson's approach was in fact quite structured, but arguments for 'free expression' gathered force within the context of the move towards progressivism in education (see Abbs 1987). Adults were encouraged to react positively to the vitality and spontaneity of children's art and teachers were exhorted to allow children's creativity to develop unhindered by their 'interference'. It seemed that the provision of materials was all that was required for children to learn.

Herbert Read's (1943) argument for the aesthetic and creative to be given emphasis in the school curriculum was developed in the 1960s by Robin Tanner (1989) and Alec Clegg (1980). Meanwhile early childhood educators, working parallel to pioneers in art education, were arguing that young children learn best through first-hand experiences, sensory stimulation and a curriculum which acknowledges the value of exploratory play. The influential Plowden Report (CACE 1967) encapsulated the spirit of the times. Of Art the authors wrote, 'Art is both a form of communication and a means of expression of feelings which ought to permeate the whole curriculum and the whole life of the school' (247).

Theories about stages of children's development in drawing (Kellogg 1969) and creative abilities (Lowenfeld and Brittain 1987) encouraged the belief that children's progression in Art was a process of natural unfolding, the result of maturation. Kellogg stated, 'In terms of spontaneous art, every child is a "born artist" who should be allowed to scribble without oppressive guidance in art education' (Kellogg 1969: 266).

In the United States Elliott Eisner challenged these ideologies, arguing that the creation and appreciation of visual art 'is not an automatic consequence of maturation but rather a process that is affected by the type of experience children have had and that a child's ability is a function of what he has learned' (1972: 105). In the United Kingdom the Gulbenkian Report (Robinson 1982) argued for a radical reappraisal of the teaching of arts, including a better understanding of the role of the teacher: 'The task is not simply to let anything happen in the name of self expression or creativity. Neither is it to impose rigid structures or ideas and methods upon the children. The need is for a difficult balance of freedom and authority' (Robinson 1982: 33).

From 1985, curriculum development in the arts, originally funded under the auspices of the School Curriculum Development Committee (1989), was continued under the National Curriculum Council for a five year 'Arts in Schools Project'. In 1990 the project culminated in the publication of 'The Arts 5–16 Project Pack'. Also during the 1980s a movement to establish 'critical studies' in both primary and secondary schools was developed vigorously by Rod Taylor and colleagues in the Drumcroon Centre in Wigan (see Taylor 1986; Taylor and Andrews 1993). They argued that children should learn about Art and artists, as well as how to produce art work of their own.

As pressures to 'sell' the school ethos and success to parents escalated in the Thatcherite climate of the 1980s, a disproportionate amount of teacher time was spent on 'window dressing'. Filling the dreaded frieze boards resulted in 'production-lines' for which little thought was given to children's gains in artistic learning. At worst, the requirement to please adult 'consumers' resulted in children spending hours sticking small squares of fabric or screwed up tissue paper in teacher drawn outlines of bunnies (spring), boats (summer), bonfires (autumn) and snowmen (winter).

Aspects of all these influential ideologies have been carried forward into the art teaching of infant teachers in the 1990s.

PRACTICES

Research evidence about the realities of classroom practice in the arts is sparse. Art is not a fundable area of enquiry in a world dominated by decision makers preoccupied with basic skills and the technical/rational aspects of education. Snippets have to be pieced together from data from HMI Reports or projects designed to investigate the primary curriculum as a whole. Evidence from the 1978 HMI survey of practice in primary schools indicated that teachers were over-whelming children with a range of 'one-off' art activities. They argued that:

> Children need to familiarise themselves with the characteristics of particular materials and to acquire some degree of mastery over essential skills and techniques. A more carefully selected range of art and craft activities, worked at more thoroughly, would enable children to reach higher standards in the execution of their work and obtain more satisfaction from it.
>
> (DES 1978: 5.95)

In 1982 an HMI survey of First School practice produced evidence that whilst 'almost half of the schools were concerned with promoting aesthetic and sensitive visual and tactile awareness in children' only 'some teachers appreciated the educational value of the work in art and craft' (DES 1982: 2.146).

Research projects in the 1970s and 1980s found that although teachers claimed to value Art, they devoted little sustained attention to teaching Art (Tizard *et al.* 1988; Bennett and Kell 1989; Alexander 1992). In the infant classrooms studied by Barbara

Tizard's team, a curious combined category called Art/Craft/ Construction accounted for 21 per cent of the ninety 7-year-olds observed working time in classrooms, whilst 3R activities occupied 64 per cent of time. Art took place during 'choosing time' or was set for a group of children to keep them 'busy' whilst the teacher focused on the demands of groups involved in literacy, numeracy or scientific tasks. In Neville Bennett's study of 4-year-olds in reception classes, Art was often 'supervised' by parent helpers or classroom assistants, but instructions from the teacher were often so vague and the purposes of the tasks so ill-defined that many adult/pupil interventions were described as 'inappropriate'. Bennett gives an example of a parent helper supervising a painting activity for which the teacher's purpose was 'colour recognition through painting'. The parent helper does not intervene when the child, Ryan, she is supervising, incorrectly names the colours of the paint several times (Bennett and Kell 1989: 66). Finally, in the Leeds City Council funded evaluation of the Primary Needs Programme by Robin Alexander, data about the teaching of Art in the late 1980s substantiated Tizard's findings. Though 6.1 per cent of pupil time was devoted to Art, many art activities were 'used to extend or round off other work ("Now do a picture") and in this respect were sometimes little more than a time-filler' (Alexander 1992: 49). The physical layout of classrooms, with practical art and craft areas frequently relegated to shared 'wet areas' between adjoining classrooms or sited away from the main area of the teacher's routine supervision, reflected the low level of teacher time allocated to Art.

There is also evidence that primary teachers lack confidence in teaching Art. This is compounded by inadequate preparation during teacher training. A study by Cleave and Sharp in 1986 found that most PGCE courses in Art were 20 hours or more and B.Ed. courses ranged from 12 to 40 hours. This contrasts with the compulsory 100 hours (under 1994 DFE regulations to be increased to 150 hours) allocated to English, Mathematics and Science training. Teachers whose own art education often stopped at the age of 13 felt insecure about their lack of personal practical Art skills.

They also felt anxious about interacting with children involved in the expression of personal ideas in Art. A student quoted in an NFER follow-up study of the training needs of primary teachers (Sharp 1990) said, 'the arts are concerned with you as a person, your emotions. In the expressive arts it's very hard to hide behind something . . . it's so personal, it's very sensitive' (69). This lingering sensitivity to the personal nature of art activities means that the history of non-intervention in Art is perpetuated.

There is little support in schools to allay these anxieties. Guidelines for teaching Art are patchy in primary schools. Art coordinators tend to be Main Professional Grade status and, interestingly, likely to be female and from Key Stage One (see Alexander 1992: 35). They lack the time and status to support colleagues.

In the Interim Report (DES 1991) review of current art education provision in primary schools the evidence was summarized as:

> Surveys by Her Majesty's Inspectors (HMI) reveal that all the classrooms visited have some form of work in art included in the curriculum. A small number demonstrate outstanding work, the majority tackle some aspects adequately, but in about a third of the classes the work is poor. In general, the work of the younger pupils is better than that of the older ones. In many schools, art has a low status and perceived value. Often insufficient time is provided, the work is poorly planned, the tasks lack adequate challenge and little attention is given to the sequence of lessons or progression and continuity. In general the work is poorly matched to the abilities of individual pupils.
>
> (3)

THE NATIONAL CURRICULUM COUNCIL ART ORDER

This was the context into which the Statutory Orders for Art were delivered to schools for a September 1992 start at Key Stage One. There were two Attainment Targets (ATs):

> AT1 Investigating and Making – the development of visual perception and the skills associated with investigating and making in art, craft and design
>
> AT2 Knowledge and Understanding – the development of visual literacy and knowledge and understanding of art, craft and design including the history of art, our diverse artistic heritage and a variety of artistic traditions together with the

ability to make practical connections between this and pupil's own work.

(DES 1992)

A ratio of 2 : 1 in favour of practical work was required for delivery and assessment of the Programmes of Study. Teachers were urged to plan for the two ATs as complementing each other. Art, Music and Physical Education, unlike other subjects, had End of Key Stage Statements rather than a 10 levels of attainment framework for assessment.

What did Key Stage One teachers make of the Statutory Order? There is evidence from a project (Clement 1993) designed to investigate the readiness and training needs in Art of primary teachers of how teachers *claimed* they would cope. Of 936 teachers who responded to questionnaires (sent to 2,000 primary schools in 22 LEAs in England and Wales), 61 per cent of teachers were positive about the Order, 24 per cent were cautious, and 15 per cent were negative. Those who welcomed the Order did so for the following reasons:

 (i) it provides a framework for planning and progression
 (ii) it raises the profile of the subject in primary schools
(iii) it will have an impact upon the range and quality of work undertaken in primary schools
(iv) it will lead to a better match between the teaching of Art and the needs of children
 (v) it will lead to children having a better understanding and knowledge about the work of artists, craft workers and designers (Clement 1993: 26).

In response to questions about structures within schools to support the new requirements, 82 per cent of schools had a curriculum leader for Art (again the majority from Key Stage One) and 56 per cent had art policy documents. When asked about their preparation to implement the order, 64 per cent of generalist class teachers claimed they had received little or no in-service training, whilst 9 per cent of curriculum leaders claimed they had received sufficient training, but 25 per cent had received none at all! All the teachers expressed anxiety about their ability to assess children's achievements and to identify their progress in Art. They were also worried about their own lack of personal/professional expertise to teach AT2, about the paucity of information books to support this aspect of the curriculum and about the costs of visiting galleries or paying artists to work in schools.

Of 88 Key Stage One teachers surveyed in the PACE project at Bristol (Pollard *et al.* 1994; see Chapter One), 54 per cent were found to be teaching less Art in 1992 because of the demands of the History, Geography and Technology Orders. They also claimed that Art was being used to 'service' National Curriculum based topics and that it was now 'less fun' to teach.

In Jim Campbell's study of curriculum reform at Key Stage One (Campbell and Neill 1994; see Chapter One), infant teachers claimed to be allocating 9 per cent of curriculum time to Art in 1992 and 8 per cent in 1993, though policy guidance was for 7.5 per cent. These data are at odds with the PACE findings. However, in Campbell's study in 1993 only 36 per cent of Key Stage One teachers believed that they had been able to allocate 'sufficient time' to Art (as opposed to 50 per cent who made that claim in 1992). He argues that the discrepancy between actual time claimed to be spent on Art and perceptions as to whether this was 'sufficient' is attributable to the teachers' growing resentment about the dominance of the 'cognitive' over what Campbell defines as 'the body and soul' subjects: Music, Art, Physical and Religious Education.

Are Key Stage One teachers and their pupils doing anything different in Art, as a result of the Order? My experience of working with teachers at initial, in-service and Higher Degree levels has highlighted some changes as well as problems carried forward from legacies already outlined. These will be explored in the remaining sections of the chapter.

ATTAINMENT TARGET 1

The strands set out in the Non-Statutory Guidance of the original Order gave teachers the security of knowing what was expected of pupils. In AT1, 'Investigating and Making', four strands were spelled out:

- recording what has been seen, imagined or remembered
- gathering and using resources and materials
- using different materials and techniques in practical work
- reviewing and modifying work.

The third strand, using different materials and techniques, may appear the most straightforward. In the Programmes of Study there are six features covering a range of techniques: line and tone, colour-mixing, pattern and texture, shape, form and space, and 3D work. The problem is that teachers have not been trained to plan activities focused on one or more of these features of Art, or to design a series of tasks for children which will build competence and understanding in a systematic way. They can find it difficult to escape from the 'one-off' or 'topic serving' rationale for Art. If we return, for example, to the teacher in the Bennett study of 4-year-olds who wanted Ryan to learn colours, she could plan a series of colour mixing activities using a limited selection of powder paints over a few weeks. First, two types of blue and a white could be set out and children encouraged to experiment with mixing light and dark blues, making patterns on paper, talking to each other and an interested adult about the thickness or thinness and colours of the paints. Similar activities could be set up with reds and yellows. Then children could be given two primary colours with which to experiment. Gradually the children's understanding of how to mix paint, make colours, use brushes, and create patterns would be developed so that they could bring this knowledge to freely chosen painting activities. The recently produced support materials from Bob Clement (1994) in video and guideline format are helpful in planning for progression.

One of the positive changes I have observed is that Key Stage One teachers are realizing that alongside free exploration of paint, clay, textiles, etc., there is a place for teaching skills and techniques – how to mix colours, texture clay surfaces, make different stitches. They are feeling less inhibited about demonstrating the appropriate use of tools and equipment – large brushes for colour washes, fine for detail; how to use pine cones to texture clay; the advantages of using large, blunt needles for weaving and fine, sharp needles for sewing.

However, set against a matrix of structured learning experiences, it is equally important that each child is given opportunities to explore mark-making as a means of making sense of the world on a personal level. Strand One, recording what has been seen, imagined or remembered, provides a framework for this personal voyage of discovery. Matthews (1987), drawing on Athey's work on schema, argues that each child develops symbolic systems in his or her attempts to capture and understand information they feel to be essential. We need to be receptive to what their marks 'stand for'. Such awareness comes only from close observation and dialogue with children as they work. Buckham (1994) gives a good example in

Carol Aubrey's book on the teaching of subjects at Key Stage One. The drawing of a monster was one in a series Jasvir had made:

> He drew enthusiastically, chuckling and grimacing at his drawing, talking to himself and to the student about it. 'It gobbles people up', he announced to her between exclamations of 'look!' and 'look at him now!' as he added dots to the surface of his drawing. He wrote 'dirty monster' above the drawing and pointed to each of the four letter symbols as he read it back to himself. As he handed over his drawing when he had finished he warned the student to be careful that she didn't get her hands dirty. She looked surprised and he explained that the monster lived in the mud and was 'all dirty'.
>
> (Buckham 1994: 135–6)

A collection of children's mark-making, dated and with teacher and pupil comments recorded, can provide evidence of 'processes of artistic growth' impossible to gain from the study of single context free drawings. As Matthews points out, psychologists have paid scant attention to such 'an important level of early representation and expression', but so have teachers. We do need to pay attention to the motives for children's drawings, as well as the factors that influence their nature. We need to construct additional models of the development of mark-making to complement a stages framework, such as Kellogg's, which presupposes a limited view of 'progression' as moving towards increasing accuracy and visual realism. Detailed studies of children's drawings at home and school, similar to those of children's emergent writing, would help us to develop such models.

Marion Wilkinson, in an article in the National Foundation for Art Education Journal, gives an example of how a sensitive teacher can build upon children's direct experience to explore their schema representations:

> One Monday morning a boy brought in a selection of shells he had collected at the weekend during a visit to the beach. Some children noticed the spiral marking on some of the shells and I asked the children to make a spiral shape in the air with their fingers. A week of making spiral patterns followed using a variety of materials. The children made spirals with pencil, crayon, paint, glue covered with sand, plasticine and clay, Multilink mathematics apparatus, large wooden bricks and coloured sticky back paper. We also cut out spirals to make

mobiles, observed the water going down the plug hole, ran in spiral patterns and all joined hands in a line to make a large spiral shape. On Monday morning some of the children had found difficulty in drawing a spiral; by Friday they were all experts! Since this exercise spirals continue to pop up in the classroom in patterns and paintings, play in the bricks and plasticine.

(1990: 12)

Strand Two, gathering and using resources and materials, capitalizes on children's natural inclination to collect things – leaves, badges, model cars, bits of 'precious jewellery', cereal packet gadgetry. This strand also reminds teachers to build up visual resources for reference – pictures of types of vehicles, animals, people, buildings – collected from magazines, comics, catalogues and pasted into scrap books. These visual resources can encourage children to develop the habit of using their referencing skills for visual as well as verbal information. Children can be enlisted to help collect interesting fabric and paper scraps for collage work. Sorting and sifting, with an adult to talk to about texture, colour, shape and size and to help practise assembling collage designs before the glue is slapped on the backing paper, will develop children's vocabulary, confidence and powers of aesthetic judgement.

The fourth strand, reviewing and modifying work, raises the spectre of 'interference in children's creativity'. 'Lovely, dear' addressed over the teacher's shoulder to a child approaching from the easel with a dripping painting, followed by a sharp 'Put it in the corridor to dry', has never been convincing. Young children know well enough when praise is deserved and when it is meaningless. If teachers allocate some attention to practical art work, it is possible for them to encourage children to talk about and modify their work as they are actively involved in doing it. Moreover, children can learn themselves how to work for improvements. Conversations, even termly, about the choice of art work to be stored in a child's folder can offer opportunities to review their achievements over time so that children and teacher can gain a sense of what has been achieved and establish new goals.

ATTAINMENT TARGET 2

Teaching AT2, 'Knowledge and Understanding', has proved both stimulating and daunting for Key Stage One teachers. Those with an interest in visual literacy have welcomed opportunities to discuss Art, Craft and Design with children. They have drawn on personal collections of postcards (see Allen 1990), taken children into art galleries (Taylor and Andrews 1993) or invited artists into schools (NFAE 1989).

As each child develops their own personal representational systems – through role play, mark-making, verbalization – they also absorb society's imagery from the context in which they are raised and educated. Some teachers have interpreted the brief to develop visual literacy with children as an invitation to explore book illustrations, advertising symbols and logos, comic strip styles, and photographs. More rare have been those brave enough to recognize the significance for future generations of ideas and information communicated through electronic images and used television or computer games or software. Many teachers are reluctant to accept the brashness and raw energy of the images of the 1990s and turn to the tried and tested images of their own preferences. All over the country, I have found children solemnly copying from postcards Van Gogh sunflowers or Monet waterlilies. It is easy to understand why this is happening. When the idea of 'critical studies' is so new to primary teachers they are tempted to play safe. But the view of Art as the product of dead, white, male, European painters is a gross distortion of twentieth-century children's daily exposure to cultural models of Art and Design as they watch television, read comics, play computer games and absorb the signs and symbols of the commercial world.

The idea of children 'copying' Great Art, particularly from small scale reproductions, makes me uneasy. I see that it makes children look carefully at the reproduction, but it does not necessarily help them to understand how the artist worked. A postcard version of a section of one of Monet's huge paintings of waterlilies can never be a substitute for the gasp you hear as people walk into the basement of the Orangerie and respond to the scale and daring of Monet's real paintings. The value of gallery visits and artists in residence in schools is that children can feel what it is to make Art – the scale, the media, the commitment of it all. Barrett (1989) argues that requiring children to copy or even work in the style of selected artists restricts their individual expression and creativity and guides them towards prescribed outcomes. He argues that it is more productive for teachers to cue into the way artists have tackled technical or representational problems as children are producing their own work. A child struggling to represent a sky could be encouraged to go and look at a book about landscapes. This approach helps children 'to make connections between their own work and that of others' and yet allows their responses to be open ended.

The movement to invite 'real' artists and crafts people into primary schools to demonstrate how they do their own work and then to encourage the children to try new techniques and media has boosted the quality of art work in some schools in quite spectacular ways. Artists have no preconceptions of what young children can and cannot do and children can respond to new expectations with unreserved energy and enthusiasm. But some residencies have been chaotic and unproductive, leaving artists, teachers and children with ragged nerves. Teachers need to liaise closely with the artists and try to tune into their way of working. They need to think ahead and organize time for groups of children and space for potentially 'messy' activities (with promises to the caretaker that it will be sorted out at the end of the project!). It is particularly important to find out whether the artist employed to work with Key Stage One classes has had experience of young children. Given these provisos, I have seen good artists in school projects boost the confidence of both staff and children in what they can achieve in Art.

ASSESSMENT

Monitoring and recording children's progression in Art continues to perplex teachers. The simplest system is for each child to have folders of their work, reviewed regularly and shared with parents and children. There are statutory requirements to record and report annually to parents children's progress based on accumulated evidence related to End of Key Stage Statements. In the original Order the statements were so vague as to be almost useless. For example, for AT2, the end of Key Stage One statements required children to be able to

(a) recognize different kinds of art
(b) identify some of the ways in which art has changed, distinguishing between work in the past and present and
(c) to make connections between their own work and those of other artists.

How could teachers assign children to a category 'has achieved end of key stage one level' or 'has failed to achieve end of key stage one level' on the basis of these vague statements? What use would a parent or Year 3 teacher be able to make of this information?

Assessment in the arts has been bedevilled by the difficulty of putting into words the aesthetic and creative aspects of achievement. A research project led by Malcolm Ross (Ross *et al.* 1993) explored models of assessing the personal/intuitive aspects of a child's achievements. They recommended that teachers set aside regular time to talk with pupils about their work. Ross argued defiantly against mechanistic forms of assessment: 'For many children assessment means enduring a form of mental and emotional derangement, the morbid exchange of a warm, living experience for a cold, dead reckoning' (Ross *et al.* 1993: 168). Quoting Schön (1983) he argued that a genuine dialogue between teacher and pupil encourages children to become 'researchers into their own practice' and so engage 'in a continuing process of self-education' (Ross *et al.* 1993: 299) towards aesthetic understanding.

It is much less complex to define skills that pupils may be expected to gain and media/techniques in which they may achieve growing levels of competence. Clement and Page (1992) have offered a useful model with examples of children's artwork set against criteria used to identify levels of achievement. They also give a matrix for checking levels of achievement across the components of the original Art Order. This kind of system, linked to children's individual folders of work, would provide an effective class and individual record keeping system.

In the Revised Art Order the End of Key Stage Statements were reduced to 11 prose descriptions. The intention was to 'simplify' the curriculum and assessment procedures, particularly for primary teachers. For example, for AT2, Key Stage One children should be able to 'describe and compare images and artefacts in simple terms. They recognize differences in methods and approaches used and make links with their own art, craft and design work' (DFE 1995: 9). I am not convinced that these revised descriptors will prove to be any more useful in helping teachers to assess achievements.

THE POST-DEARING ART ORDER

One of the more helpful aspects of the revised Order is that a direct relationship is drawn between the Programmes of Study and the End of Key Stage Statements. The Programmes of Study are clearly set out as a guide to curriculum planning for each key stage. In AT1 the strand 'gather resources and materials, using them to stimulate and develop ideas' is expanded in key stage specific statements as:

At Key Stage 1: AT1 (b) recognise images, objects and artefacts as sources of ideas for their work

At Key Stage 2: AT1 (b) use sketch book to record observations and ideas and to collect visual evidence and information for their work

At Key Stage 3: AT1 (b) select and record observations and ideas and research and organise a range of visual evidence and information, using a sketchbook.

(SCAA 1994)

These statements provide a clearer framework for teachers to plan an art curriculum within and across key stages.

There is an enhanced policy on provision for children with special educational needs. For the small number of pupils who may need the provision, material may be selected from earlier or later key stages. Such material should be presented in contexts suitable to the pupil's age. Appropriate provision should be made for pupils who need to use:

- means of communication other than speech, including computers, technological aids, signing, symbols or lip-reading
- non-sighted methods of reading, such as Braille, or non-visual or non-aural ways of acquiring information
- technological aids in practical and written work
- aids or adapted equipment to allow access to practical activities within and beyond school.

Art education may be entering a phase when what children do in primary schools is more systematically planned and monitored than ever before. Yet resistance to changing practice in education is always stronger than policy makers expect. As Eisner (1988) argued, 'Ideas, even good ideas, without tenacious support, both financial and moral, have a hard time surviving when they belong to a field that has historically been regarded as educationally marginalised.' Key Stage One teachers now have the possibility of using the revised statutory Order to justify, resource and teach good quality Art education for the benefit of their pupils. I hope they will do so.

REFERENCES

Abbs, P. (1987) Towards a coherent Arts aesthetic, in Peter Abbs (ed.) *The Arts in Education*. Lewes: Falmer Press.

Alexander, R. (1992) *Policy and Practice in Primary Education*. London: Routledge.

Allen, D. (1990) The Duchess of Portsmouth: A project in visual art/media education in the first school, *Visual Education*: 10–13.

Athey, C. (1990) *Extending Thought in Young Children, A Parent-Teacher Partnership*. London: Paul Chapman Publishing.

Barrett, M. (1989) Correspondence in *NSEAD Newsletter*, January–February. Coventry: University of Warwick.

Bennett, N. and Kell, J. (1989) *A Good Start: Four Year Olds in Infant Schools*. Oxford: Basil Blackwell.

Buckham, J. (1994) Teacher's understanding of children's drawing, in Aubrey, C. (ed.) *The Role of Subject Knowledge in the Early Years of Schooling*. London: Falmer Press.

Campbell, J. and Neill, S. (1994) *Curriculum Reform at Key Stage 1, Teacher Commitment and Policy Failure*. Harlow: Longman for Association of Teachers and Lecturers.

CACE (Central Advisory Council for Education) (1967) *Children and their Primary Schools* (The Plowden Report). London: HMSO.

Clegg, A. (1980) *About Our Schools*. London: Blackwell.

Clement, R. (1993) *The Readiness of Primary Schools to Teach the National Curriculum Art*. Plymouth: Rolle Faculty of Arts and Education, University of Plymouth.

Clement, R. (1994) *Understanding Progression in Primary Art, Planning for Progression In Primary Art and Reviewing Progression in Primary Art*. Exmouth: Centre for the Study of the Arts in Primary Education.

Clement, R. and Page, S. (1992) *Principles and Practice in Art*. Harlow: Oliver and Boyd.

DES (1978) *Primary Education in England: A Survey by H.M. Inspectors of Schools*. London: HMSO.

DES (1982) *Education 5 to 9: An Illustrative Survey of First Schools in England*. London: HMSO.

DES (1991) *National Curriculum Art Working Group Interim Report*. London: DES.

DES (1992) *Art in the National Curriculum*. London: HMSO.

DFE (1995) *Art in the National Curriculum*. London: HMSO.

Eisner, E.W. (1988) Structure and magic in discipline-based Art education. *Journal of Art and Design Education*, 7(2): 185–6.

Kellogg, R. (1969) *Analysing Children's Art*. Palo Alto, CA: Mayfield.

Lowenfeld, V. and Brittain, W.L. (1987) *Creative and Mental Growth*. New York: Macmillan.

Matthews, S. (1987) The young child's early representation and drawing, in G.V. Blenkin and A.V. Kelly (eds) *Early Childhood Education. A Developmental Curriculum.* London: Paul Chapman Publishing Co.

Pollard, A., Broadfoot, P., Croll, P., Osborn, M. and Abbott, D. (1994) *Changing English Primary Schools? The Impact of the Education Reform at Key Stage One.* London: Cassell.

Read, H. (1943) *Education Through Art.* London: Faber and Faber.

Robinson, K. (1982) *The Gulbenkian Report. The Arts in Schools: Principles, Practice and Provision.* London: Calouste Gulbenkian Foundation.

Ross, M., Radnor, H., Mitchell, S. and Bierton, C. (1993) *Assessing Achievement in the Arts.* Buckingham: Open University Press.

Schön, D.A. (1983) *The Reflective Practitioner: How Professionals Think in Action.* Aldershot: Averbury.

Schools Curriculum and Assessment Authority (1994) *The National Curriculum Orders.* London: SCAA Customer Services.

Schools Curriculum Development Committee (1989) *The Arts 5–16: A Curriculum Framework.* Harlow: Oliver & Boyd.

Sharp, C. (1990) *Developing the Arts in Primary Education: Good Practice in Teacher Education.* Slough: NFER.

Tanner, R. (1989) *What I Believe: Lectures and Other Writings.* Bath: Holborne Museum and Crafts Centre.

Taylor, R. (1986) *Educating for Art: Critical Response and Development.* Harlow: Longman.

Taylor, R. and Andrews, G. (1993) *The Arts in the Primary School.* London: Falmer Press.

Tizard, B., Blatchford, P., Burke, J., Farquar, C. and Plewis, I. (1988) *Young Children at School in the Inner City.* Hove: Lawrence Erlbaum.

Tomlinson, R.D. (1947) *Children as Artists.* London: Penguin.

9 | MUSIC

David Dawson

WHAT IS MUSIC EDUCATION IN PRIMARY SCHOOLS?

There are many popular images of Music in the primary school. The
most common are those centred around the activity of singing in one
form or another, although whole class recorder playing (descant
recorder, of course) and listening to three or four pieces of
nineteenth-century music with vivid images or story lines, will evoke
strong memories for many people. Even the media seems to have a
collective memory. No television documentary or radio play with a
primary school setting appears to be complete without shots and
sounds of well-scrubbed, happy-faced children singing. If the singing
is enthusiastic and even a little untuneful, so much the better. Such is
the media cliché. It says, without need of further comment, that we
are in a primary school. This cliché is, by definition, over-used, but it
is not without some truth and so it has acquired this symbolic role.
Children singing has achieved this logo-status because for many
people outside education, and not a few inside it, young children
singing *is* music education in the primary school.

Of course children *should* sing, and the National Curriculum in
Music says so. (Key Stage One: 'sing songs from memory, developing
control of breathing, dynamics, rhythm and pitch' and 'sing unison
songs . . . developing awareness of other performers'.) Hopefully,
children will enjoy singing, as well as become better singers,
but music education has far richer implications. The National

Curriculum in Music sets a framework for children's education through Music. That framework is to promote educational development, aural awareness and the skilful use of the primary musical resource – SOUND – through the three musical activities of performing, composing and listening.

The content of the National Curriculum is by no means revolutionary. Its emphasis on practical involvement with sound has its roots in the frequently quoted Hadow reports of the 1930s, whilst children as composers generated much interest and enthusiastic disciples from the mid-1960s. The wider soundscape of non-Western musics and popular cultures grew in significance in music education in the 1980s.

All the significant features of the National Curriculum in Music had been announced well in advance – some by decades. This is not to say that all schools adopted these developments, indeed there is evidence that there is a wider variety of provision for Music than for any other area of the curriculum. The HMI report, *The Teaching and Learning of Music* (DES 1991), highlights this: 'the content of the music teaching and the quality of the musical achievements of the children varied considerably within and between the schools', and in specific activities 'most children had experienced the fundamental activities of listening to and performing music, but only in about half the schools was there any opportunity to compose music' (DES 1991: 7–10).

In the last ten to fifteen years some LEAs, aware of the need for a more structured approach to music teaching in order to achieve coherence and progression both within and across sectors, developed guidelines for music education. Some of these have influenced music teaching well beyond their own areas. The arrival of a 'national' and statutory curriculum in Music should not have been a surprise in terms of its content; however, the level of 'surprise' will depend on the existing situation within any particular school. Whatever the level of preparedness, the National Curriculum in Music does challenge every school to provide music education to prescribed guidelines for all children. It can no longer be left to chance or governed by the particular enthusiasm, or discrete skill of one member of staff in a school.

THE IMPLEMENTATION OF THE NATIONAL
CURRICULUM IN MUSIC

The comprehensive implementation of the National Curriculum in Music at Key Stage One is, and will be, conditioned by two very important factors: existing practices in music education and a perceived view of the nature of Music in general, largely derived from the vast commercial music world.

Existing practice is the result of a historical progression whose main features are well known. Limiting a historical overview to the twentieth century it is sufficient to say, without wishing to over-simplify the situation, that for the vast majority of children large group singing and a limited listening repertoire were the dominant musical activities up to the mid-1970s, and for many children beyond this time. There have of course been other less pervasive aspects of music education in the twentieth century, all with avid followers. Percussion bands featured in some schools and there was interest in the teaching of musical rudiments, theory and notation. The teaching of descant recorder, still much maligned outside the classroom, has a presence in many schools. In the second half of the century other influences were felt, through the work of Carl Orff, in structured improvisation and the use of quality tuned percussion instruments. The legacy of Kodaly's work in music education is, for most people, the use of handsigns as visual representation of pitch, but his true legacy is the centrality of music education through the voice. Recently, children have been encouraged not just to perform and listen, but also to compose – to organize and shape sounds for an expressive purpose. Music programmes on television and radio, used frequently in schools with younger children, have reflected this widening of musical influence and activity, although the focus is still essentially on singing.

The omnipresent commercial music industry is an undoubted influence on attitudes to Music in school. Music plays a large part in most peoples' lives, pre-eminently as listeners, and thus emphasizes the notion that Music is composed by a highly talented handful, performed by a larger but still small number of gifted people, and listened to by everyone. Such a commercial view of Music too readily translates with dire consequences into Music in education. It is easy to see in a historical review how the commercial music view has impinged on Music in school. Music in education, or better still, education through Music, takes a quite different standpoint and the full implementation of the National Curriculum in Music would emphasize the equal value of listening, performing and composing.

ORGANIZATION OF MUSIC EDUCATION

The way a school organizes its music education clearly has a significant bearing on the nature and quality of that musical experience. The assumption has been that, with children at Key Stage One, the class teacher would make provision for *all* curriculum areas through work in specific subjects and through topics and projects. In general this happens, and for some teachers Music is an important feature of their curriculum planning. But frequently Music does *not* feature in the class teacher's whole curriculum provision. The reason is not hard to find. If music education is largely singing, then the organizing and leading of this requires musical skills on the teacher's part: the abilities to sing in order to demonstrate the song, to read music (unless the song is familiar), to play an accompanying instrument (guitar or more usually the piano) to provide support.

Even with young children, the tradition developed of Music being taught not by the class teacher, but by the 'specialist' – defined in many cases as 'a pianist'. There are many examples where the visiting pianist is responsible for the total music education of young children. This may be effective music education, but it is more likely to be simply an enjoyable time for teacher and children, without structured development and progression in musical skills and understanding. Allen (1989) sees real dangers in the dominance of piano accompanied singing: 'reliance on the piano can easily inhibit activities such as unaccompanied singing, instrumental work, creative work and attempts at integration. While teachers are able to use the pianist as a prop they probably feel less need to undertake any real curriculum and professional development' (Allen 1989: 152). The piano-centred music specialist is unlikely to provide the best framework for implementing either the wide content or the exploratory nature of the Key Stage One National Curriculum in Music.

The National Curriculum in Music was implemented at Key Stage One in 1992. The relatively late arrival of a statutory provision plus the inherited patterns in music education point to a very varied provision for children at Key Stage One: some will be receiving very little in the way of music education, others, probably the majority, will be receiving a restricted music education based on singing and listening, and a third group will be exposed to a wide range of musical activities. The National Curriculum in Music is designed so that the music education offered to the third group of children will become the normal pattern.

In the National Curriculum there are six strands covering the three areas of musical experience: performing, composing, listening and appraising. At Key Stage One children will be expected to both sing and play, and in so doing develop the ability to control sounds and take initial steps in associating them with signs. In composing, children will be encouraged to explore a wide range of sounds, to improvise and, through selecting and organizing sounds, to express ideas and images. Mills (1991) stresses the universality and availability of composition: 'Composing takes place whenever a person (or a group of people) devises a piece of music. It may use the resources of a full symphony orchestra, or three chime bars' (Mills 1991: 23). Whilst much of the early work will be directly using the raw material of music – sound – children should have opportunities to explore how they can be 'stored' through the use of simple symbols – the beginnings of notation. The listening programme should help children progressively to become more aurally perceptive – to be able to listen with increasing objective clarity in order that their subjective view can be properly supported. It is expected that children will encounter a wide soundscape with 'music in a variety of styles . . . from different times and cultures' (DFE 1995). There is no limit to the kind of music that can and should be used in music education. The only questions to be asked are: Will this music serve a positive purpose? Will it enhance aural awareness? Will it be purposeful listening?

COPING WITH CHANGE

Clearly the full implementation of the National Curriculum in Music will, for many teachers and schools, involve considerable changes in practice, attitude and resourcing. Some of the changes may be easily made. Others, particularly those involving the changing of attitudes and the development of new teacher skills and confidence, will take much longer. But a start has been made, firstly in recognizing that change is necessary, and secondly in the provision of resources and staff training. The simplest task is to build up resources. Money is now being used to provide a wide range of instruments to support work in Performing and Composing. Easier access to instruments with non-Western origins makes this a potentially exciting area.

Music is being given some priority in individual school in-service programmes as the gap between present provision and future needs is addressed. Even a short in-service course can provide a sufficient shift in understanding of music education for a teacher to start exploring aspects of music education that had previously been considered beyond their capability.

Whilst some progress is being made through in-service work, two perennial problems exist:

(a) a narrow understanding of the purpose of music education
(b) a lack of confidence in working practically with sound.

Holt (1989) characterizes this situation as 'conceptual confusion, operational passivity and professional indifference', and further adds 'lack of confidence in this area is identified as a particular difficulty' (Holt 1989: 146–51).

There are a number of ways the Key Stage One general class teacher can be supported and encouraged to be involved more fully in music education. For some teachers the use of a planned scheme of music education will provide a structure (e.g. Silver Burdett, 1989). But even the best schemes demand flexible use and the ability to depart from the scheme according to the particular needs or contexts in which it is used. This flexibility is available to those with some expertise in the subject. Lack of expertise often results in a limited number of 'model' lessons being available and an inability to move beyond these. For some schools the strategic use of a music coordinator or specialist working alongside class teachers can build up sufficient technical support and reassurance.

It may be that the key question for the full implementation of the National Curriculum in Music at Key Stage One is simply: how *can* the general class teacher acquire the knowledge and confidence to engage in a wide range of music learning activities with their pupils? Some recommendations can be offered:

• by establishing within the school a clear understanding of the role of Music in education
• by not trying to emulate the methods of the music specialist, but instead working in those areas and with those activities that have a less demanding technical role for the teacher. This would include

composing, games to develop aural awareness and a wide listening programme with children

- by accepting that the widest possible soundscape is available for music education. There is no limit to what can be used and the non-specialist may grow in confidence if he or she works initially with simple non-traditional sounds (body sounds, sounds using natural materials) and music that is familiar
- by putting creative work – composing – in a central position and accepting that it is available to all children and manageable by all teachers
- by recognizing that music is sound and that any notation of that sound is not 'the music' but only a way of representing and storing that sound.

This final point needs emphasizing because many teachers justify their lack of confidence by virtue of their inability to read music – that is to handle notation. It is important to realize that much of the early work in both composing and performing need *not* involve notation. Early musical experience is concerned with working directly with sound – with discovering, handling, controlling and shaping sounds – before thinking about the need to represent sounds with some form of notation. There is a clear parallel here with language acquisition. It is also worth remembering that much of the world's music does not involve notation. There will come a time when there *is* a need to hold or store a sound – perhaps so that further work can be done in composition or so that someone else can perform a composition. The National Curriculum acknowledges this need and at that point various forms of notation can be explored.

Because of the still prevalent use of a music specialist, even at Key Stage One, there is a tendency to put music education into large timetable slots often in the hall or a 'music' room. The fact that Music can be noisy and resources may have to be shared contribute to this need for timetabling. There may be practical reasons for long but infrequent periods for Music, but there are problems associated with this organization. Music teaching is likely to be most effective for the general class teacher when it is taught in short sessions, with varying sizes of groups according to the activity, and at appropriate times of the day. There might be a two-minute game developing pitch awareness, the listening to, clapping of, and feeling for a steady pulse, the adding of sounds to a story, the singing of a song linked to a topic or project, simply listening to sounds within and outside the classroom, exploring different qualities of sounds for a class assembly on 'contrasts'. Such, and similar activities, are the most effective patterns for music education at Key Stage One. Much, if not all of the requirements of the National Curriculum in Music, can be effectively delivered in this way by the general class teacher.

Whilst advocating a strong musical role for the non-specialist, the support of someone with more formal musical skills may be necessary for the general class teacher to be an effective music educator and to grow in confidence. The role of the consultant or curriculum leader is clearly one of importance and needs defining. It is not a specialist who takes over, but rather supports and enables other teachers. The consultant may handle certain activities which call for specific and specialized technical skills on the teacher's part, but the main role is support. This support may be technical advice, suggestions for suitable repertoire, assisting in the development of the class teacher's own musical skills, and above all, helping to build confidence.

THE WAY FORWARD

Much in-service music provision has been directed at the primary level. Teachers will have gained from the courses some personal music skills (recorder playing, singing) and had new musical experiences (composing, improvising). They will be able to replicate some of the activities with their children. But three questions remain. Firstly, having done these new activities with my children, what do I do next? Secondly, how do I assess the success of these activities for both teacher and children? Thirdly, what do I do if the unexpected happens, if children respond differently, if things 'go wrong'? These are valid questions from a non-specialist teacher. The third question is as much to do with teacher confidence and attitude to learning in the arts as having specific musical skills and knowledge to deal with problems. In all the arts things 'go wrong' – certainly if you are taking risks and encouraging the exploration of thoughts and feelings in creative work. With confidence such occasions can be seen not as problems, but as springboards to imaginative responses and potential starting points for new developments – the very heart of creative work.

The first two questions are generated by a proper demand to plan for progression and to be able to evaluate and assess progress. In the

National Curriculum in Music Order it was claimed that the curriculum would make 'progression more explicit both across and within key stages'. It is difficult to see how this is achieved *within* a key stage. The Programme of Study is written not in terms of developing and increasing understanding and skill, but in simple statements of what pupils should be *taught* (e.g. at Key Stage One 'explore, create, select and organize sounds in simple structures').

Ensuring progression *across* the key stages is made more explicit, thanks to common General Programmes of Study, but even here it is expressed in the broadest of terms. Thus, for the Key Stage One example given above, at Key Stage Two the specific Programme of Study statement is: 'explore, create, select, combine and organise sounds in musical structures'. The statements can only be considered as markers along the road of musical development from 5 to 14 years. To achieve these markers teachers will need to plan for progression. In so doing they should be aware that in Music, individual progression is unpredictable, and it is not always necessary to be offering new activities and experiences. The Music Advisers' National Association commends Bruner's concept of the spiral curriculum as appropriate for music education:

> Planning a spiral curriculum might take the form of a series of experiences based either on imaginative or technical topics providing opportunities for pupils to be introduced to musical concepts and to become involved in a process of 'revisiting' them throughout their school careers. On each occasion the intention would be for pupils both to bring past experiences to bear and to gain new insights.
>
> (Music Advisers' National Association 1986: 22)

Assessment is closely associated with progression. If progression is achieved by revisiting experiences via a spiral curriculum approach, assessment is made easier in that we are observing and assessing progress between two attempts at similar experiences separated by time. At Key Stage One children are to be taught, as part of composing, to communicate musical ideas to others, using notations. These well might be simple graphic notations, at first meaningful only to the composer. With experience in this activity the graphic notation may develop so as to be capable of storing sound that others might interpret. That progression can, over a period of time, be assessed. There will be some scope for more focused assessment of progress in aural awareness and performing skills but with most music education based on practical group work, observation will probably be the single most important mode of assessment. Ogilvie (1992) writes that assessing musical development 'must rest largely on the observational skills which good practitioners already possess to a high degree' (Ogilvie 1992: 204). Assessment is, of course, made easier if the initial aims of activities are clear, and that will happen only if there is a real understanding of the fundamental purposes of music education.

What is the realistic expectation of music education at Key Stage One for the future? Nobody can pretend that the arrival of a National Curriculum in Music will or can change quickly and radically the provision for music education for young children. Existing patterns of provision are deep rooted both in style and content but, there is much to play for . . . and sing, compose and listen for! The statutory framework is in place and it has widespread support as the way forward. But, it is only a signpost to the future; the road has to be travelled, the map made, and the skills and confidence developed by teachers in order to journey forward. There is evidence that there is a growing commitment to the changes that will be needed. It is unlikely that we shall see a dramatic nationwide conversion. With persistence, little by little, music education at Key Stage One will change, so that it will be a vital and enriching part of all children's education and an indispensable component of all teachers' work with young children.

REFERENCES

Allen, S. (1989) Case studies in music consultancy. *British Journal of Music Education*, 6(2): 152.

DES (1991) *The Teaching and Learning of Music*. London: HMSO.

DFE (1995) *Music in the National Curriculum*. London: HMSO.

Holt, D. (1989) Grasping the nettle: the arts in the primary school, in M. Ross (ed.) *The Claims of Feeling: Readings in Aesthetic Education*. London: Falmer Press.

Mills, J. (1991) *Music in the Primary School*. Cambridge: Cambridge University Press.

Music Advisers' National Association (1986) *Assessment and Progression in Music Education*. MANA.

Ogilvie, L. (1992) Key Stage-Struck! Assessment and class music making. *British Journal of Music Education*, 9(3): 204.

10 PHYSICAL EDUCATION

Carolyn Jones

Physical Education is the only foundation subject compulsory from 5 to 16 years. To some extent this is an acknowledgement of its educational importance, but its value is more widely recognized. A powerful sports lobby has emerged who stress the social and cultural significance of sport, especially team games (Duke of Edinburgh 1994; *Hansard* 1994; *The Guardian* 1 March 1994). Additionally, a recent government White Paper, *The Health of the Nation* (DoH 1992), reported problems arising from the passive life-style of many of today's citizens. There is now anxiety about the low level of activity of pre-adolescent children in England (Sleap and Warburton 1994). Thus, there is common concern across the departments of Education, Health and Heritage to reaffirm the value of Physical Education, although the form it may take may be defined differently by each of these interest groups.

Physical Education in schools is a subject with a high profile but a low status. It was one of the last Orders to be implemented – in August 1992 – and no sooner had it been introduced in a slim form, than the Dearing Review in December 1993 required that it be trimmed by a further 25 per cent.

The development of Physical Education at Key Stage One will be influenced by its status in the curriculum, and the demands of having to deliver the whole National Curriculum. This chapter will:

- examine the particular role of PE at Key Stage One
- review the PE Order

- identify the views of some key personnel on the current state of PE in primary schools
- look at the future of the National Curriculum in PE at Key Stage One.

THE ROLE OF PHYSICAL EDUCATION AT KEY STAGE ONE

The essence of PE at Key Stage One is to learn to move: to move to grow and to move to learn. Its unique contribution to the education of this age phase may be expressed in the following aims:

- to promote the physical growth and development and active health of children aged 3–8 years
- to develop physical competency and psycho-motor learning through gymnastics, dance and games (and athletics)
- to promote the integration of the whole person (Phenix 1964).

According to Arnold (1968) 'the body improves with use and regresses with disuse'. Exercise is known to be of benefit to normal growth and development, specifically to the six bodily systems: cardio-vascular, neuro-muscular, skeletal-muscular, respiratory, excretory and digestive. Armstrong and McManus (1994) argue that activity patterns and positive attitudes to exercise are laid down in the early years. The National Curriculum PE should therefore encourage health-related activities for this age phase.

In terms of physical competency and psycho-motor learning, the curriculum is based on developing inherited basic motor patterns to mechanical efficiency. These may be categorized as:

- *Locomotor* movements such as crawling, walking, running, jumping, climbing, rolling, hopping, bouncing and skipping
- *Axiel or non-motor* movements such as bending, stretching, twisting, turning, sitting, lying, standing, swinging, hanging, swaying, pushing and pulling
- *Perceptual-motor or manipulative* movements such as throwing, catching, kicking, heading, striking, aiming and propelling
- *Fine motor skills* such as cutting, sewing, drawing and writing.

If all these motor patterns are practised and developed, even at a rudimentary level, each child should progress in Physical Education. However, to reach the required level of mechanical efficiency, the skills must be taught, used and developed within different activity contexts and extended into outdoor and adventurous activities, such as the soft-playroom and swimming, since variety of usage is crucial to ensure skill diversification and adaptation. According to Sugden (1990) all the physical skills children will ever have are present in a 7-year-old. Future learning in sport, physical recreation and dance are, therefore, all dependent upon the quality of basic motor patterns and bodily fitness established at Key Stage One.

According to Tanner (1978) the processes of intellectual, emotional and physical development are inter-dependent. Since physiologically the sensory motor and perceptual motor areas of the brain develop ahead of the rest, Physical Education can provide an accessible vehicle for developing thinking and feeling, thus encapsulating within a single subject thought, feeling, sense and action (Phenix 1964).

THE PHYSICAL EDUCATION NATIONAL CURRICULUM AT KEY STAGE ONE

The post-war years saw the introduction of a movement-based programme of Physical Education (Bray 1992). The principles of movement – weight, space, time and flow – were developed by Rudolph Laban. Most Physical Education is presented as class lessons, but the pupils are expected to work on the activities set at their own rate and pace and at their own level of capability. This ensures that late and early developers (Tanner 1978) and those with special educational needs are all catered for. A standard response from the whole class is *only* expected when basic motor patterns are being practised or skills taught. The whole thrust of a movement-based physical education programme is to provide for differentiated outcomes. The National Curriculum PE was based on these principles and is essentially a process curriculum (Kelly 1989).

The new Order (SCAA 1995) is slimmer but the basic approach is retained. There are three core activities – games, gymnastics and dance – through which the cognitive processes of planning and describing and the physical process of performing are to be promoted. Planning to cover the Programmes of Study should take account of themes to be covered, tasks to be set and skills to be taught. Children's achievement will be reported annually with reference to End of Key Stage Descriptors. For Key Stage One they are:

Pupils plan and perform simple skills safely and show control in linking actions together. They improve their performance through practising their skills, working alone and with a partner. They talk about what they and others have done and are able to make simple judgements. They recognise and describe the changes that happen to their bodies during exercise.

(SCAA 1995)

This Level 2 standard of achievement, embedded in the four descriptors, is expected of most 7-year-olds.

There remain some unresolved areas of concern for implementing the Key Stage One PE curriculum:

- the credibility of the revised Order with its reduction to three activities, reduction in the core content in gymnastics (shape and space) and dance (the dynamics, making dances, and using a range of stimuli for creative work)
- the manageability of delivering the Order in the identified 36 hours per year allocation
- the status of the subject
- the quality of teaching and the question of standards.

PERCEPTIONS OF TEACHERS ON THE CURRENT STATE OF PHYSICAL EDUCATION

Since the school is the focal point for addressing these concerns, it was felt to be pertinent to secure the views of those directly responsible for implementing the new order at Key Stage One – Reception and Years 1 and 2 class teachers, PE curriculum leaders, headteachers and an Inspector. This was done with semi-structured interviews (transcribed) in three schools (two primary and one first) in an inner city LEA, where two of the schools were in areas of social deprivation. The schools were known to the author through earlier research on provision, and through Initial Training and In-service links. For obvious reasons it is not possible to generalize from these findings, but they may provide insights into the future development of PE at Key Stage One and a yardstick against which to conduct a school policy review.

The findings

Credibility

Despite the reductions in Outdoor and Adventurous Activities and Athletics, there were no concerns about the viability of the subject for Key Stage One amongst school staff. All felt confident that the foundations of PE could be effectively taught through the three core activities. In one case 'teacher time' had been allocated to continue to offer outdoor and adventurous activities. In each case swimming would be offered at Key Stage Two.

However, the Inspector felt that the integrity of the subject had been undermined by the removal of two unique areas of physical experience from the Statutory Order, although it was accepted that schools may still chose to offer them and the problem of curriculum overload *was* acknowledged.

Manageability

There were no real concerns about the delivery of the curriculum. There was some debate about the new requirement to teach competitive games at Key Stage One. Although the principle of competition was supported, it was considered unproductive to introduce competition and group work before individual skills were fully established. Concerns were expressed about phase specialists also having to offer expertise to children in dance and games. It was seen as unrealistic to expect so much of one teacher.

School staff felt confident about delivering the PE curriculum within the time allocation of one-and-a-half-hours per week for two of the schools and two hours for the other. However, they anticipated a sharper focus on planning and timetabling to make the best use of the time available. Two of the schools were planning to introduce a modular system to ensure coverage and to respond to the seasons. Outdoor games and athletics would be intensively pro-grammed in the summer term and first half of the autumn term to make the most of better weather. In one school the problems of the provision of time for changing, as well as for training in putting out and putting away apparatus, has been accommodated by time-tabling one hour for gymnastics and outdoor games in the summer and one half hour for dance and indoor games. In another school an 'apparatus day', with a rolling programme of classes having responsibility for putting out *or* away the equipment, covered this aspect of training effectively. In the third school, the core activities were taught weekly to ensure regularity of exercise and continuity in skill training; and apparatus training for gymnastics and games was integral to the work of each session. The question of depth as well as coverage was only raised in one school where PE was to be a daily lesson for everyone.

The issue of assessment had not been addressed and whilst there was relief at the lack of formal requirements to assess PE, there was interest in a diagnostic system which would help inform the planning of the next stages of teaching and learning for children.

In general these findings reflect OFSTED (1994) findings that Key Stage One teachers were positive about the PE Order and could teach it to a satisfactory or better level.

Status of the subject

The headteachers acknowledged the value of a quality programme of PE and had supported their teachers through INSET provision, reasonable time allocations for PE, a good level of funding and resources, and lively after-school programmes in PE for Key Stage Two children. In the two inner-city schools, parents raised funds for PE. In the urban school, the headteacher had allocated PE as a particular responsibility to a governor.

In all three schools there were Early Years units for the 3 to 5-year-olds. They had a wide-ranging PE programme based on play for the nursery children and core physical activities with a play and skill acquisition basis in the reception classes. There were no tensions between reconciling the needs of the 5-year-olds and the non-statutory school age children within the same groups. The teachers in the Early Years units were all well-versed in the PE Order. Thus from the age of three children were given opportunities for a 'runabout' which would lay the foundation for their PE development in future years.

All the teachers encouraged school sport and forged relationships with outside agencies and experts. They felt PE was a high-profile subject which, in an era of open enrolment, enhanced the recruitment of pupils to the school. All those interviewed stressed that the subject needed to be vigorously promoted to encourage *all* schools to prioritize PE.

Quality and standards

The most recent report by OFSTED (1993) rates the teaching of the PE National Curriculum at Key Stage One as generally satisfactory to good. However, these judgements of quality were mostly made by generalists rather than those with a PE or Activity specialism. Judgements of good standards would be based on the children's ability to plan, perform and describe in games, gymnastics and dance. The quality of teaching and learning in PE is acknowledged to be influenced by: teachers' knowledge and expertise; their commitment to planning and assessment; the approaches used to develop the subject; adequate time allocation to PE; levels of funding and resourcing; and an enrichment programme of after-school provision using both school and external personnel. Each of the three schools surveyed believed that they *did* provide a quality PE curriculum at Key Stage One which included many of the features commended by OFSTED.

The schools also believed that it was essential for PE sessions to be observed as part of the OFSTED inspections. A section of the OFSTED handbook is devoted to evaluating the quality of PE programmes (reference to standards of achievement on page 42, the quality of learning on page 43, accommodation for PE activities, resources, teaching and learning on pages 90 and 91). For the first time there is now a framework for the systematic monitoring of PE in primary schools, albeit that the monitoring may be only as good as that provided by a generalist team of inspectors, without necessarily including expertise in PE.

The Inspector expressed reservations about the quality of Initial Training. An article in *The Guardian* (13 September 1994) refers to unpublished research from Exeter University indicating that in some PGCE courses students get only four hours of training in PE, and in some four-year courses as little as twenty hours, and also that there is little in-service in PE for practising teachers. Clearly this lack of training creates problems for the generalist Key Stage One teacher.

Concluding views

Despite the difficulties of convincing every teacher in their schools of the value of offering a quality PE curriculum to all children, all the respondents, and especially headteachers, remained convinced that PE would retain an important place in the infant curriculum. They felt that curriculum leaders were crucial to the future development of the subject. However, as advisers became inspectors, the loss of their expertise to support improvements in PE at Key Stage One was considered to be significant. There was also anxiety about how schools would continue to meet the costs of resourcing the curriculum – especially to pay for swimming lessons at Key Stage Two and the costs of buying and maintaining equipment which inevitably suffered hard wear and tear.

All the respondents believed that the class teacher rather than a specialist, as happens in Scotland, was the best person to teach PE. They also believed the school should retain control over any use of outside personnel, both to safeguard the children and to maintain control over the quality of experiences offered to children.

THE WAY FORWARD

Some problems remain. Inevitably, with core subjects having priority at Key Stage One, there is a glass ceiling on what is possible in PE. Additionally, though there are clear benefits to a class teacher system, there will always be limitations in their subject knowledge and expertise. Employing specialists does not seem a workable solution at Key Stage One.

There are other national developments. A new blueprint for school sport is being planned by Ian Sproat with strong backing from the Prime Minister (see *The Guardian* 13 September 1994). A National Junior Sports Programme (the National Coaching Foundation) with commercial sponsorship was launched in March 1995 by the Youth Sports Trust, a charity set up by the Sports Council. Its aim is to develop sporting programmes for 4 to 18-year-olds. Children at Key Stage One (4–9) will be provided with 'Top Play' – programmes of games activities, with resources and activity theme cards – for a wide variety of volunteer outside personnel to use with children. This initiative has highlighted the need for the education sector, especially headteachers, to plan how schools might lead and manage such programmes. In conclusion Physical Education at Key Stage One must remain primarily the responsibility of schools. It is 'the child that counts, not the activity' and it is teachers who are most familiar with the needs of young children.

REFERENCES

Armstrong, N. and McManus, A. (1994) Children's fitness and physical activity. A challenge for PE. *British Journal of Physical Education*, 25(1): 6–10.

Arnold, P.J. (1968) *Education, P.E. and Personality Development*. London: Heinemann.

Bray, S. (1992) Towards the national curriculum – a review of developments in PE in primary schools in England and Wales during the twentieth century. *Bulletin of PE*, 28(3): 7–25.

DoH (1992) *Health of the Nation. A Government White Paper*. London: HMSO.

Duke of Edinburgh, HRH (1994) Statement on PE. *British Journal of Physical Education*, 25(1): 6–10.

Hansard (1994) The Queen's Speech to the Commonwealth, April 1994.

Kelly, A.V. (1989) *The Curriculum: Theory and Practice*. London: Paul Chapman.

OFSTED (1993) *Physical Education. Key Stages 1, 2 and 3. First Year*. London: HMSO.

OFSTED (1994) *A Handbook for Inspection*. London: OFSTED.

Phenix, P. (1964) *Realms of Meaning*. USA: McGraw-Hill.

SCAA (1995) *Physical Education in the National Curriculum*. London: SCAA.

Sleap, M. and Warburton, P. (1994) Physical activity levels in pre-adolescent children in England. *British Journal of Physical Education*, Research Supplement, 14: 2–6.

Sugden, D. (1990) Development of physical education for all. *British Journal of Physical Education*, 21(1): 247–57.

Tanner, P.J. (1978) *Education and Physical Growth*. London: Hodder and Stoughton.

11	RELIGIOUS
	EDUCATION
	Eileen Bellett

The changes introduced by the Education Reform Act reflect
the Government's commitment to strengthening the position
of Religious Education and collective worship in schools.

(DES 1989: 4)

As a professional working in the Theology department of a Higher
Education institution, with a background in primary teaching and a
specialism in Religious Education, there has been an unprecedented
demand for my services during the last few years. The 'demand' has
provided me with opportunities to work not only with undergradu-
ate students on teacher training courses, but also with a variety of
teacher groups in the northern region, through professional development days, INSET and short courses in conjunction with individual
schools, LEAs and local dioceses. This chapter draws on dialogue
with these networks of teachers to consider the ways in which Key
Stage One practitioners have interpreted the legislation and developed teaching and learning strategies in Religious Education.

Having placed the continuing Religious Education debate in a
historical context, this chapter will go on to outline the legislative
requirements of the 1988 Act and subsequent government guidelines
and examine the effect of these on the on-going debate about
Religious Education and the way in which schools are responding.
The chapter will focus on the following key issues:

- the status of Religious Education as a subject in the basic
curriculum

- the relationship between Religious Education and other curriculum areas
- planning Religious Education as a separate subject or as part of a cross-curricular theme
- the place of world religions in Religious Education
- assessing Religious Education.

The chapter will conclude with a consideration of whether or not there has been a significant enough shift in attitude to Religious Education to be optimistic about its future.

THE BACKGROUND 1944–88

Statutory requirements are not new in Religious Education. The subject has suffered from the 'compulsory tag' since the 1944 Act set down a requirement that Religious Education should be provided for all children in maintained schools as recognition of the vested interest of the Church in the state education system in the UK. The current prevalence of negative attitudes towards Religious Education can, in part, be traced back to this legislation. To be told that a subject is required in law does not, in itself, provide the necessary motivation for effective teaching. This was certainly the case in Religious Education. A feeling of resentment developed towards the subject which has continued to the present day. Teachers aware of the statutory requirement, but lacking confidence, question not only their own approach to the teaching of the subject but also the right of the subject to exist at all. The model of Religious Education which underpinned the 1944 Act was a model based on Religious Instruction and not Religious Education. Although the Act was not explicit in requiring 'instruction in the Christian faith', it was generally assumed this was what was required. Consequently, many teachers felt unable to engage in an activity which they perceived to be evangelical rather than educational. Furthermore, the confusion about the nature and purpose of the subject led teachers to question their own involvement in something in which they did not personally believe.

Clearly, Religious Education did not remain static in the intervening years between the 1944 and the 1988 Education Acts. As with other areas of the curriculum, research into the development of children's thinking, and in particular the development of children's religious thinking, influenced the development of Religious Education. The work of Ronald Goldman in the 1960s was probably the most influential and resulted in a 'life-themes' approach which attempted to root children's learning in experience. Goldman's (1964) contention, that most 'Bible teaching as such would appear to be wasteful and inappropriate with . . . younger children' (Goldman 1964: 232), resulted in the inclusion of Bible stories as part of the primary curriculum being viewed with suspicion in some schools. However, some thirty years on, many teachers still have an approach which consists in the main, of 'telling a Bible story, writing about it and drawing a picture' (Goldman 1964: 232).

Religious Education, post-Goldman, continued to reflect wider changes in society, education and theology. As British society became more obviously diverse, incorporating many cultures and many faiths, this was reflected in theory at least in the development of a multi-faith approach. The Schools Council (1977) report *Discovering an Approach* advocated Religious Education that is:

> *Plural* in the sense that it is not restricted to one tradition
> *Open* in the sense that the scope of the subject and its content are not defined from within one religious tradition
> *Exploratory* in terms of the attitude it encourages on the part of children and teachers
> *Aimed at Understanding* and so concerned with the development of capacities and attitudes, the exploration of important ideas, and the imparting of factual information.
> (Schools Council 1977: 8)

The liberalizing of theology and the accessibility of theological ideas through the media enabled people to question 'truths' which had previously been accepted as given. The effect of these societal, educational and theological changes was the development of an approach to Religious Education which was educationally based, multi-faith in content and interactive in approach. A cursory glance at the writings of Religious Education specialists such as those involved in the Westhill Project in the period up to the passing of the 1988 Act confirms this (see Read *et al.*1986; also Wood 1989). However, the persistence of negative attitudes, the confusion about the nature and purpose of Religious Education, the lack of confidence in the teaching of world religions and a widespread inability to translate Religious Education policy into good practice meant that although changes were indicated in the writings of specialists, these changes rarely filtered through into primary classrooms.

THE 1988 ACT

The 1988 Act re-enacted the requirements of the 1944 Education Act but also introduced new requirements for Religious Education and Collective Worship. The following extract offers a useful summary of the Religious Education clauses:

> Unchanged
> - there must be provision for Religious Education for *all* pupils
> - the Religious Education provided in county schools must be non-denominational and must still be in accordance with a locally agreed syllabus prepared by a Conference set up under Schedule 5 of the 1944 Act
> - the parental right of withdrawal is unchanged
> - so are the safeguards for teachers who do not wish to participate in or conduct Religious Education
>
> Changes
> - new locally agreed syllabuses must reflect the fact that religious traditions in the country are in the main Christian whilst taking account of the teaching and practices of other principal religions
> - whilst Religious Education must be non-denominational in county schools, the new law makes it clear that teaching *about* denominational differences is permitted
> - Standing Advisory Councils on Religious Education (SACREs) *must* be established, according to a specified composition, and with extended general functions
> - SACREs *may require* an LEA to set up a Conference to review the locally agreed syllabus
> - the composition of such Conferences is amended
>
> (DES 1989: 2–3)

The guidelines outlined in the government circular of January 1989 provided the definitive framework for the interpretation of the legislation until January 1994 when the Department of Education Circular 1/94, incorporating both the statutory requirements of the 1988 and the 1993 Education Acts on Religious Education and

Collective Worship, superceded it. The main additions from the 1993 Act focus on the provision for grant-maintained schools and subsequent amendments to the composition of SACREs and Standing Conferences, the review of syllabuses and arrangements for the inspection of Religious Education. There continues to be a degree of controversy about some of the wording in the circular and further confusion about its status. Many teachers believe that this circular 'replaced the Act' and constituted a mandatory document. However, 'the circular sets out the Government's policy on Religious Education and collective worship in schools, and gives guidance to those concerned with these matters . . . This guidance does not constitute an authoritative legal interpretation of the Education Acts.' (DFE 1994:10).

MODEL SYLLABUSES

Following the publication of draft model syllabuses in the early part of 1994 the final versions were distributed to schools in September. The comment of a Key Stage One teacher, 'I hear the North Yorkshire syllabus has been scrapped now and replaced by the model syllabuses', was typical of teachers' reactions. The background to the development of these syllabuses was a perceived deficiency in the approach to the teaching of world religions. This was deemed to be particularly prevalent at Key Stage One where, it was claimed, children were being confused by being introduced to a 'mish-mash' of faiths as part of cross-curricular topics on, for example, celebration. It was not uncommon, the critics maintained, for children in the Early Years to be actively engaged in 'faith-hopping' as several festivals from the world's major religions were visited in turn. Two model syllabuses were produced, each taking a different approach:

Model 1. Living Faiths Today
Model 2. Questions and Teachings

The model syllabuses attempt to provide a structured approach to teaching about world religions which respects the integrity of each faith. The response from teachers has been confused. As with Circular 1/94 there has been a general misconception about the status of these documents. Most have not grasped that 'the models are ... guidance'. The media almost entirely ignored this point. The documents are the result of wide consultation and a great deal of painstaking work but they have no legal authority for the Religious Education curriculum.

(Rudge 1994)

Working with primary teachers on courses, I have identified a mixed response to the model syllabuses. Some welcome them as 'filling a gap', whilst several teachers have welcomed the 'prescriptiveness' of the models and the comprehensive guide to progression. However, Key Stage One teachers have not responded so positively and have expressed concern about the level of knowledge and understanding expected of young children. They believe that the expectations do not reflect how young children think and learn. Some of these concerns echo those expressed following the publication of earlier Agreed Syllabuses. For example, commenting on a statement of attainment from the North Yorkshire syllabus for Key Stage Two, one teacher stated 'Know the names of six world religions – I couldn't do that myself'.

What evidence is there that the statutory requirements are being translated into good primary practice at Key Stage One?

SUBJECT STATUS

Religious Education is part of the basic curriculum. It is not a foundation subject but has the same status, although it is not subject to the same requirements for assessment. The government (DES 1989: 4) in confirming the 'special place of Religious Education' claims to be committed to 'strengthening the subject'. The debate continues as to whether this strengthening could have been more effective had Religious Education been part of the National Curriculum. In talking to teachers, I am clear that more of them are aware of the importance of Religious Education and that there is an increasing recognition that Religious Education is a valid discipline in its own right. However, the placing of Religious Education in the basic curriculum, and yet not as a foundation subject, exacerbates the problem of status.

In the last few years funding has been made available for Religious Education designated courses aimed at enhancing subject specialism and developing leadership skills. There has been no shortage of application to those LEAs in the North who have offered such courses. As course tutor, I could be encouraged by this interest and conclude that, at long last, the subject is receiving the recognition it deserves. However, my experience of working with Religious Education coordinators does not confirm this. The reasons given for becoming a Religious Education Coordinator are revealing in themselves:

> The school was part of an LEA re-organisation . . . we all had to indicate which areas we'd like to be responsible for.

> There was only Religious Education left when the list reached me . . .

> I did a bit of Hinduism in my degree course – I wasn't main Theology or Religious Studies but my headteacher seemed to think the Hinduism was good enough for me to be Religious Education Coordinator.

> All my staff are already over-worked, no-one would do Religious Education so, as the Head, I took it on.

> The choice was Religious Education or Physical Education . . . I took the Religious Education. I was never very good at games.
> (Key Stage One teachers, Leeds)

A similar 'tale of woe' surrounds the attitudes of staff with whom the coordinator has to work. In response to the question, 'which aspects give you greatest concern?' the following replies indicate that the status of subject is not yet clear in the minds of some teachers:

> Some staff have opted not to teach Religious Education – it's left to a part-time teacher.

> I still have to get teachers to accept it is important to teach Religious Education.

> There is a lack of interest, a lack of expertise. How can I change this?
> (Key Stage One teachers, North Yorkshire)

A course which offers Religious Education coordinators time to develop their specialism, and more importantly time for reflection, is clearly one way of enabling those who have positive views about the status of Religious Education to disseminate this to others.

PLANNING RELIGIOUS EDUCATION

One of the clearest outcomes of the advent of the National Curriculum has been the growing acceptance of the need for more rigorous planning. Has this been evident in Religious Education? Unfortunately, a good deal of planning in Religious Education is still *ad hoc*, an after-thought or an appendage even in schools where there are policies. A headteacher in Leeds recently offered me this observation: 'We have a new agreed syllabus; we have a school policy but we still don't know how to do it – I mean if the topic is Water, we still write down Noah's Ark.'

At Key Stage One it is very likely that Religious Education will be delivered as part of a cross-curricular topic. The danger is that Religious Education will either disappear or lose its distinctiveness. The Bible story approach outlined earlier is also still evident.

Taking a group of students into a Year 1 class recently, I was asked by the class teacher whether I thought the students would benefit from hearing her 'aims' for Religious Education. I replied that this would be helpful. 'Religious Education,' said the class teacher, 'is about getting on with each other. If we can be more caring and sharing then I feel we've done a good job'. There is, inherent in this statement a fundamental confusion about the nature and purpose of Religious Education. For some Key Stage One teachers there is no distinction between Religious Education and Moral Education. Indeed Moral Education is probably the acceptable face of Religious Education. Key Stage One teachers often feel more comfortable with this kind of approach as it is part of the ethos of the Early Years classroom. It does not demand specialist knowledge of either religion or religions and can consequently be approached without anxiety. The result is often the negation of Religious Education as a subject. Religious Education it is claimed is 'going on all the time' and does not, therefore, need to be planned but simply recorded if, and when, it happens.

A further 'planning weakness' also stems from a view which equates Religious Education with Collective Worship: 'We do our Religious Education in assembly'. Although government guidelines usually deal with Religious Education and Collective Worship in the same document, this should not be interpreted as indicative that the two areas are synonymous.

If Religious Education is to be taught in a cross-curricular way, care must be taken to ensure that it is planned in the same way as other contributory subjects. There needs to be a clear set of learning outcomes. Teachers need to think through what it is that they want children to know and understand. Learning activities should be devised which will enable children to achieve the learning outcomes. There should be a sequence of learning with differentiated tasks for the more able and those with learning difficulties. The criteria for determining 'special needs' in Religious Education are not necessarily the same criteria employed for other curriculum areas. Special needs in Religious Education may include children with a marked potential to develop empathy; children who appear unable to express their feelings; children whose faith background makes particular demands on their time and commitment; and children whose family background prevents them from exploring religions in an open manner. Clear strategies for the assessment, recording and reporting of the Religious Education component need to be in place.

THE WORLD RELIGIOUS ISSUE

Local agreed Religious Education syllabuses for county schools and equivalent grant maintained schools must in future reflect the fact that religious traditions in the country are in the main Christian whilst taking account of the teaching and practices of other principal religions.

(DFE 1994)

There has been a growing acceptance that world religions should be included as part of the Religious Education curriculum. The legislation does not make specific requirements about particular faiths at the various Key Stages. However, a principle adopted by most LEA Agreed syllabuses and Diocesan syllabuses is that by the end of Key Stage Two children should have had the opportunity to study in depth, Christianity and no more than two further world religions 'The syllabus further recommends that, especially at Key Stage One and Two pupils should not attempt to study more than two faiths in depth in addition to Christianity' (Manchester Diocesan Board 1994: 7).

Prior to 1988, there was a degree of hesitancy on the part of Key Stage One teachers about teaching world religions. This stemmed partly from a lack of teacher knowledge, partly from a general viewpoint that it would 'confuse' the children and partly from a perception that teaching about world religions is only necessary in certain geographical areas. The report *Education for All* published in 1985 (DES) had clearly had little impact. One of the observations of this report was that the multi-faith content of Religious Education could make a significant contribution to multi-cultural education. However, although Religious Education specialists had recognized this potential, it had largely been ignored by practising teachers. At Key Stage One, teaching about world religions is often confined to Christianity and Diwali. The inclusion of Diwali as part of the learning experience of Key Stage One children has almost reached epidemic proportions. The festival has tremendous potential for art, music, drama and language. A headteacher in North Yorkshire gave a typical view: 'Religious Education is just starting to be given consideration but we have looked at the theme of Diwali as a whole school and the parents were supportive'.

The 'Diwali tendency' has led, however, to the perpetuation of age-old problems for Religious Education. How can we avoid repetition, how can we plan for progression and how can include world religions in a way which both respects the integrity of each religion but includes material that is relevant to the age and aptitude of young children?

As indicated earlier in this chapter, the model syllabuses may prove to be a useful resource to enable teachers to organize concepts, skills and attitudes in a coherent fashion. More importantly, however, schools will need to agree about 'which religions when' and plan to deliver these over the Key Stages to ensure a broad, balanced and coherent Religious Education curriculum.

ASSESSMENT

Those LEAs which produced their syllabuses soon after 1988 debated loud and long about whether or not to adopt the language and structure of the other National Curriculum documents. Should the agreed syllabus, for instance, include Attainment Targets, Programmes of Study and Statements of Attainment? Or is Religious Education so distinctive that the National Curriculum structures are inappropriate? Several years on, it is interesting to note that the majority of new syllabuses have adopted a National Curriculum model to ensure parity with other subjects.

The next step on from this debate is the question of assessment. Should Religious Education be assessed? Is it possible to assess learning in Religious Education? Assessment is, of course, related to planning and once teachers accept that Religious Education involves planned learning outcomes and structured learning activities, it is not difficult to accept that appropriate strategies can be devised to assess these.

The assessment issue is currently at the top of the agenda – mostly, it must be admitted, as a response to impending inspection. However, at the time of writing, there is still a lot of groundwork to be done. Most Religious Education policy documents cross-reference the assessment issue to the school assessment policy, but there is little evidence that learning in Religious Education is being systematically assessed.

THE WAY AHEAD

This chapter has painted a rather depressing picture. The overall impression is that there continues to be a gap between policy and practice. There has been a proliferation of policies in anticipation of inspection but in some cases policies are written, at the request of senior management, by the curriculum coordinator and involve little shared understanding with the rest of the staff. For Religious Education to be properly implemented there must be a real sense of policy ownership. Misconceptions about the nature and purpose of Religious Education are still widespread and where the Religious Education coordinator can be given time to work with staff towards a shared philosophy of Religious Education this can only be beneficial – far better to have a 'developing policy' than a finished product which is rarely implemented.

The enhanced provision of Religious Education designated courses aimed at developing subject specialism and improving leadership skills bodes well for the future. The response from a Key Stage One teacher to defining her post-Dearing professional development needs is both timely and salutary: 'To provide day-time courses (centrally funded) . . . Ban all twilight courses . . . we have families too!'

The opportunity to share issues of common concern on a centrally funded day-course enables coordinators committed to Religious Education to think through their own philosophy and devise strategies to combat the negative attitudes of teachers in their schools.

At a recent Religious Education Coordinators course, teachers were outlining the way in which Religious Education was delivered in their own school. One colleague commented:

> There was no Religious Education to speak of in our school, so I was appointed on a part-time basis to write a policy and work out how Religious Education could 'fit into' the topic cycle. I've done this and now take responsibility for teaching the Religious Education slot in all the classes. The only thing is, when I arrive to take Religious Education the class-teacher walks out.

This school has solved the problem of Religious Education not happening. However, the strategy has been unsuccessful in changing teacher attitudes to the subject. The report *Education for All* (DES 1985) outlined the need for teachers to undergo a fundamental re-orientation of attitude if multicultural education was to be taken seriously. The same is true for Religious Education. It is not sufficient that teachers are required to teach Religious Education but rather that they be committed to teaching it as a subject which is educationally worthwhile.

REFERENCES

DES (1989) *The Education Reform Act 1988: Religious Education and Collective Worship*, circular 3/89. London: HMSO.
DES (1985) *Committee of Inquiry into the Education of Children from Ethnic Minority Groups. Education for All* (The Swann Report). London: HMSO.
DFE (1994) *Religious Education and Collective Worship*, circular 1/94. London: HMSO.
Goldman, R.J. (1964) *Religious Thinking from Childhood to Adolescence*. London: Routledge and Kegan Paul.
Manchester Diocesan Board of Education (1994) *Syllabus for Religious Education*. Manchester: Church House.
Read, G., Rudge, J., Teece, G. and Howarth, R.B. (1992) *The Westhill Project, R.E.5–16, How Do I Teach R.E.?*, second edition. Cheltenham: Stanley Thornes.

Rudge, J. (1994) New syllabuses for old?, in *Westhill R.E. Centre Update*. Birmingham: Westhill College.

Schools Council (1977) *Discovering an Approach*. London: Macmillan Education.

Wood, A. (1989) *Religions and Education*. London: West London Institute of Higher Education.

<table>
<tr><td rowspan="5">12</td><td>THE WAY AHEAD:</td></tr>
<tr><td>ANOTHER NATIONAL</td></tr>
<tr><td>CURRICULUM FOR</td></tr>
<tr><td>KEY STAGE ONE?</td></tr>
<tr><td>Angela Anning</td></tr>
</table>

THE DEARING REVIEW: AND ANOTHER NATIONAL CURRICULUM

Throughout the period of reform, relationships deteriorated between the teaching profession and successive Secretaries of State thrown up by Cabinet re-shuffles. John Patten succeeded in uniting every sector of the deeply conservative profession – maintained and independent, primary and secondary, pre-school and primary, Higher Education and school, headteacher and teacher unions – into revolt. In 1993 English teachers in the secondary sector spearheaded a formidable and articulate attack on the prescribed content and procedures of the proposed SATs for 14-year-olds. Teaching unions' power had declined throughout the 1980s and 1990s, but in 1993 they used their remaining influence to coordinate primary and secondary teachers' refusal to carry out the statutory tests for 7-year-olds and 14-year-olds. The unions won a court case which ruled that the teachers' actions were legal because the statutory requirements of assessment had resulted in unreasonable workloads.

Early Years teachers began to demonstrate a new confidence. In the same year as the boycott of the SATs, they mobilized parental and political support against Patten's 'Mums' Army' scheme. He proposed to set up one-year training schemes for non-graduates 'with a couple of A-levels' to teach children up to the age of seven. Doug McAvoy, General Secretary of the National Union of Teachers, voiced the concern of Early Years educators that the proposals 'were underpinned by a false and offensive assumption that teaching young children is easy, requiring fewer professional skills and less personal education' (Reported in *The Independent* 10 June 1993). The speed and professionalism with which early childhood educators lobbied for support against the scheme marked a new 'with-it-ness' in a group of workers pushed to their limits. The willingness of parents to rally in support of their children's nursery and infant teachers appeared to take the Minister by surprise.

It was not the only example of ministerial misreading of parents' views. The central notion of parents as 'consumers of education' was enshrined in a Parents' Charter (DES 1991) which set out their procedural rights. Parents were given rights to express preference for a school of their choice, to receive an annual written report on their child and to have access to league tables of the performance of local schools, a school prospectus, an annual governors' report and regular reports on schools from the inspectorate. In the White Paper, *Choice and Diversity: A New Framework for Schools* (DFE 1992) the official line was that 'Parents know best the needs of their children – certainly better than educational theorists of administrators, better even than our mostly excellent teachers' (DFE 1992: 2). Yet when representatives of Parent-Teacher Associations, representing eight million parents, lobbied Patten in opposition to the national league table publication of SATs results, he dismissed them as 'Neanderthal'. Two research studies of parents' actual rather than perceived views on primary education during the period of reform, based at Exeter University and reported in Hughes *et al.* (1994), indicated that they were reluctant to see themselves as consumers. What emerged was that parents were far more interested in 'human' than procedural aspects of schooling. They valued factors beyond academic results – notably that the school was a friendly, welcoming place where teachers, pupils and parents had good relationships with each other and where their child would be happy. In fact, 85 to 90 per cent of parents said that they were satisfied with their children's schools. Their only complaint was that they wanted more information about what their children actually did in school so that they could be more directly involved in helping them.

In 1993 the popular Chief Education Officer of Birmingham, Tim Brighouse, whom Patten had described as a 'nutter', won a symbolic court victory when his accusation of slander was upheld. While Patten subsequently nursed a viral infection, Baroness Blatch of Hinchinbrooke was drafted in to preside over a radical re-think of the reforms. Sir Ron Dearing, a man who had presided successfully over conflict at the Post Office and seen to be 'a safe pair of hands', was appointed to oversee a review. He began an exhaustive and effective programme of consultation with teachers resulting in an Interim Report (Dearing 1993a). Horrified to discover that primary teachers had to deal with 966 Statements of Attainment to deliver the statutory curriculum, he set up a series of working parties with both subject and Key Stage briefs, to rationalize the Orders and related assessment requirements. Within four months a Final Report was ready for consultation (Dearing 1993b).

By May 1994, SCAA had drawn up draft, slimmed down Orders. Sir Ron boasted that the primary curriculum, to be collated for the first time in one complete document, was now 'one centimetre thin'. The aim was that Programmes of Study rather than assessment criteria should be used as the basis for curriculum planning. At Key Stages One, Two and Three, one day a week was to be freed up from the requirements of the Orders to give teachers more flexibility. The ten-level scale was retained, but the 966 detailed Statements of Attainment were replaced by 200 Level Descriptions. Teachers were urged not to keep detailed records of each child's progress in achieving separate Attainments Targets, but to judge which level description 'best fits' their pupil's attainments at the end of each key stage. The final version of the Orders was introduced into schools in the autumn of 1995. We have been promised five years of stability.

Arrangements for testing children at seven are to be 'simplified'. English and Mathematics SATs will be retained using a mixture of classroom tasks and paper and pencil tests covering reading, writing, spelling and number work. At Level 2 three sub-grades (A–C) will be assigned to give a greater definition to the assessments. It will be possible for an able pupil to take Key Stage Two Level 4 tests. Only these papers will be marked externally. Class teachers will mark all other tests. Four days per class of supply cover may be costed into LEA GEST (Grants for Education Support and Training) bids for the implementation of SATs. These 'days' will also have to provide time for training teachers for the new testing arrangements. The LEA costs for auditing SATs through visits to schools for moderation and scrutiny of marked papers will also have to be met from the grant. LEAs, already starved of funds from central government, will have to pay 40 per cent of the total costs to attract the 60 per cent government grant.

DILEMMAS FOR THE NEXT FIVE YEARS

The inspection of primary schools

It is now clear that the proposed system for inspecting primary schools every four years is unworkable. OFSTED is unable to cope with its legal duty to inspect all 18,000 primary schools within four years. Already there is a backlog building up. There are not enough trained inspectors, and those already trained are reluctant to bid for contracts to inspect small primary schools because the work is not economically viable. A few primary and special schools have already been thoroughly 'OFSTEDed' under a system designed for large secondary schools. Others will have to wait nervously to see what changes will be made to yet another unmanageable system set up by the government and when, or if, they are to be inspected.

The education of under-fives

The education of under-fives has become an all-party focus of political interest. An under-fives task group at the Department for Education is addressing John Major's aim, announced at the 1994 Conservative Party Conference, of providing nursery places for all 4-year-olds whose parents want them. The visionary report, *Learning to Succeed* (National Commission on Education 1993), paid for by the Paul Hamlyn Foundation, argued for 'a statutory requirement on local authorities to ensure that sufficient high-quality, publicly funded nursery education places are available for all 3-year-olds and 4-year-olds whose parents wish it' (132). Major's platform is that additional high-quality pre-school places must be targeted in a way that expands and does not crowd out the private and voluntary sector. There has been a rapid expansion in private day care, nursery schools and play groups. In 1989 The Children Act defined social services duties and powers to regulate and inspect all services for children, but the task of monitoring the quality of care and education across maintained and private day care nurseries, childminders, play groups and maintained and independent education nurseries is made difficult because of the inevitable budget constraints. In July 1995, the controversial voucher scheme was launched. Parents of 4-year-olds were to be offered vouchers worth £1,100 to spend on playgroup, maintained or private nursery 'education'. The idea is that 'market forces' will produce nursery provision that the state is unable or reluctant to finance.

However, in many LEAs the school-entry age has been effectively lowered to 4 anyway. More and more 4-year-old children start full-time school in September, even if they are only just four. They are often in large classes, above the recommended number of 26 for Reception classes, and with limited non-teaching assistant support for the teacher. Placing a 4-year-old in full-time schooling with facilities geared for 5-year-olds upwards is a poor substitute for properly resourced nursery provision. The recommendations of The Rumbold Committee, *Starting With Quality* (DES 1990), for good quality educational provision for 3-year-olds and 4-year-olds were: a staff/pupil ratio of 1 : 13; preferably half-day attendance; and a curriculum 'which emphasises first-hand experiences and which views play and talk as powerful mediums for learning' (35 : 13e). Which political party will face the costs of rescuing our 4-year-olds from well documented educational disadvantage? (Cleave and Brown 1989, 1991a, 1991b; Anning and Billett in press).

SCAA and OFSTED have been set the task of drawing up curriculum guidelines for under-fives. The National Commission argued in *Learning to Succeed* that the curriculum for 3-year-olds and 4-year-olds should be 'broadly defined and not unduly prescriptive'. It remains to be seen whether such advice will be followed.

The Code of Practice for Special Educational Needs

Schools and local authorities are also required to respond to the new Code of Practice on the Identification and Assessment of Special Educational Needs (DFE 1994a). Every school must publish information about their policies for the likely fifth of their school population with special educational needs. There must be a named SEN coordinator, to be known as a SENCO, with responsibility for implementing the policies. There are five stages defined, with time scales specified, for the identification and possible statementing of children with special educational needs. Parents must be involved at all stages and in a subsequent annual review of targets set for a child.

A Citizen's Charter Guide for Parents has been published (DFE 1994b) setting out the requirements of schools and LEAs and naming voluntary sector agencies to whom parents may go for support. Dissatisfied parents may register complaints about school or LEA provision to a regional special needs tribunal. The coordinator is likely to be asked to attend. These tribunals are expected to deal with 700–1000 cases in the first year (Bowers 1994).

There are two major problems for primary schools. First, there are few staff who possess the specialist expertise in special educational needs necessary to undertake the role of coordinator. The government has provided £7.3 million for training through GEST bids; but of course LEAs will have to contribute an additional 40 per cent to the costs of training programmes. Peter Mittler, Professor with Special Educational Needs responsibility at Manchester University, has argued that the full costs of staff development for coordinators and for teachers working with 'priority groups' – such as pupils with sensory impairments, severe learning difficulties and emotional and behavioural difficulties – should be met by central government. He believes that the government should extend requirements for mandatory qualifications, beyond those specified for teachers working with children with visual and hearing impairments, to all teachers with 'significant' SEN responsibilities (*Times Educational Supplement* 1994).

The second problem is the perennial one of time. Primary teachers have argued that the demands of the National Curriculum and assessment have already reduced the time they can spend with children with special educational needs (Lewis 1992). Without funded release from their class responsibilities, how can they be expected to respond to the additional requirements of the Code of Practice?

The training of teachers

The government initiative to base initial training in schools will also place extra demands on teachers. Circular 14/93 (DFE 1993a) sets out new criteria for courses. A diversification of routes into teaching is to be encouraged including a three-year six-subject BEd, a distance learning Open University PGCE and a Specialist Teaching Assistant training programme. Higher Education (HE) and schools are instructed to work in partnership, students to spend more time in schools and mentors in schools to take on increasing responsibility for training and assessing students. The shift of responsibilities will result in 'transfer of resources from the institutions to their partnership schools' (6.37) to pay, for example, for supply cover to release class teachers for their training role. Schools may bid to train without HE involvement.

Schools and HE institutions are working painfully towards developing new models of training as roles and responsibilities are redefined. HE staff will face redundancies as money is diverted to schools. There are problems about the economy of scale of units of training in a school-based model, since most primary schools are reluctant to take on more than two to four students. They simply do not have space for extra bodies! The issue of who will input curriculum knowledge in the new arrangements is a vexed one. HMI have argued that primary schools do not generally have the capacity or range of expertise to take on significant additional training responsibilities without considerable support. Galton (1994) cites evidence from Bennett and Carré (1993) and Summers (1994) that both primary teachers and students have significant subject knowledge gaps. He argues that the knowledge base demanded of primary teachers has become unrealistic and addressing the gaps too costly. He suggests that subject knowledge at primary school level is of secondary importance. Instead of chasing what Shulman (1986) defines as 'pedagogical content knowledge', Galton proposes that initial training, both at HE and school level, should concentrate on teaching the generic skills of 'pedagogic knowledge of teaching'. Others (for example, Alexander *et al.* 1992) propose that competencies of teachers should be divided into three groups for initial, induction and INSET stages and a formal obligation laid on those responsible for each to deliver their part of the training process. With LEA advisers in short supply and HE staff being shed, will primary teachers really be able to take on the additional burden of training responsibilities?

There is a further dilemma for Key Stage One trainers. Courses in child development and psychology have been squeezed out as the government has demanded increased hours for curriculum training. Early Years practitioners argue that child development should be a core element in training for work with young children (see Kelly 1994). Yet course designers are reluctant to differentiate between the overall content of Key Stages One and Two training programmes. It would be unwise, for example, to offer subject specialist training only to Key Stage Two students. Such differentiation would re-open the old divisions between infant and junior departments, which the coherence of the National Curriculum has done so much to break down, and limit the career prospects of Key Stage One students. Besides first employers are looking for beginning teachers with maximum flexibility in both Key Phase and Curriculum expertise.

THE WAY FORWARD

The post-modernist tendency to draw on aspects of the past to reconstruct new systems has bedevilled the last six years of curriculum reform. The very phrase 'Back to Basics' says it all. Politicians hark back to 'traditional' methods, and teachers, demoralized by attacks from the government, media and researchers, to an idealized version of Plowdenism. Who can we look to for a way forward to a curriculum fit for young children in the twenty-first century?

In the Interim Dearing Review, we were told 'The principal task of the teacher at Key Stage One is to ensure that pupils master the basic skills of reading, writing and number' (Dearing 1993a). In the Final Report the distinctive purposes of Key Stage One were redefined as

to lay the future foundation of learning by:
(i) developing the basic skills in reading, writing, speaking, listening, number and information technology
(ii) introducing young children to a broad range of interesting content spanning the subjects of the curriculum
(iii) promoting positive attitudes to learning and helping young children to work and play together harmoniously
(Dearing 1993b: 31, 4.12)

It is significant that skills in speaking, listening and information technology have been bolted on to the tired old basics of reading, writing and number. These skills will certainly be crucial for survival both in daily living and work in the next century.

Each author of the subject chapters in this book has argued cogently for the value of teaching their own subject discipline to young children. There was relief amongst Key Stage One practitioners that the gains they had made in enhancing and extending the curriculum over the last six years were not to be swept aside by a retrenchment, as some would argue for, to basic literacy and numeracy. However, in the Final Report it was made clear that reductions in content in the new slimmed down primary curriculum would be concentrated 'outside the core subjects' (ibid.: 4.3) and there have been strong hints that the one day a week freed up from the statutory curriculum at Key Stage One should be allocated to the basics. Science specialists should be concerned that the time for Science, a core subject at Key Stage One, will be effectively reduced to one-and-a-half hours per week (10 to 15 per cent of four days). This contrasts oddly with the required hour a week for Religious Education.

Beyond the mechanistic arguments about the specifics of time allocation to subjects, we need an informed and unpressurized debate about what kind of curriculum best fits the current and future needs and entitlement of young children. In response to a request from HMI to re-define the basics for a curriculum for 3 to 7-year-olds, I drew on various published models of priorities (for example DES 1985, ILEA 1987 and Blyth 1984) and my own sense of what really matters:

> The curriculum for 3 to 7-year-olds only needs to be 'retro-spective' in that it should be based on the central principle of effecting a gradual transition from what children have already learned and achieved before they enter school, to what will be the foundations of 'school learning' and hopefully lifelong 'education'. The basics should be the beginning of generating knowledge, skills and attitudes for productive lives as individuals and members of society. For me 'the basics' of education for 3 to 7-year-olds should be listed as opportunities and encouragement to develop:
> - *physical confidence and competencies* including awareness and control of their own bodies; large and fine motor skills; positive attitudes towards maintaining health and fitness
> - *interest and curiosity about interpreting and understanding the world about them*; positive attitudes towards care of the environment
> - *effective ways of communicating with others*; confidence and fluency in speech or signing; use of information technology for communication; understanding and use of conventional symbol systems
> - *literacy*; confidence in decoding texts; ability to retrieve information from hard copy or electronic systems; under-standing of the range of languages and prints available

- *numeracy*, ability to classify, sort, recognise patterns and relationships, mechanically, or through information technology; understanding of mathematical recording systems; problem solving strategies; use or recording of numbers, measurements etc. for functional purposes
- *aesthetic and creative abilities*; confidence in doing their own and appreciating creations of others in dance, drama, music, art and craft and imaginative play; freedom to experiment and make informed choices based on their own interests in the arts; confident use of storying
- *understanding of moral issues*; awareness of fairness and justice; understanding of the need for rules and systems of control; awareness of right and wrong; awareness of potential misuse of prejudice and stereotyping
- *socially acceptable behaviours*; respect for self and others; independence and self-control; conformity to the negotiated/agreed rules of their school/classroom systems
- *positive attitudes to school and learning*; sense of purpose in school activities; application to tasks; sense of personal achievements; sense of affiliation to the school and its community
- *spiritual/emotional stability*; ability to stand back and reflect; ability to come to terms with strong emotions; understanding of how their actions impinge on the lives of others; awareness of 'spirituality' in others either through religious faith or feeling for 'the significance of life'.

(unpublished paper for HMI 1994)

This kind of list may form the basis of a different kind of debate about a national curriculum for Key Stage One.

In the United States some schools have been experimenting with radically different curriculum models such as that based on Howard Gardner's ideas of teaching and learning which draw on multiple intelligences (Gardner 1993a, 1993b). Gardner argues that 'by the end of early childhood, youngsters have developed powerful and already entrenched theories about their immediate world: the world of physical objects and forces; the world of living entities; the world of human beings including their minds' (1993b: xii). This constructivist approach has been repeatedly commended within this book by the subject authors. What is different about Gardner's thesis is that he distinguishes between *intelligences*, which are human intellectual proclivities, 'part of our birthright', and *domains*, the subject disciplines, crafts and pursuits which are part of our culture. He argues:

> There is a relation between intelligences and domains, but it is crucial not to confound these two realms. A person with musical intelligence is likely to be attracted to, and to be successful in the domain of music. But the domain of musical performance requires intelligences beyond the musical (for example, bodily kinesthetic intelligence, personal intelligence), just as musical intelligence can be mobilised for domains beyond music in the strict sense (as in dance or in advertising). More generally, nearly all domains require proficiency in a set of intelligences; and any intelligence can be mobilised for use in a wide array of culturally available domains.
>
> (1993b: xxi)

Gardner believes that the education system does not capitalize on the impressive cognitive and affective powers of 5-year-olds' minds but instead alienates them from learning by focusing on a narrow range of their intelligence – notably the linguistic and logical/ mathematical – ignoring six other important forms – musical/ auditory, visual/spatial, kinesthetic, interpersonal, intrapersonal and intuitive/spiritual. The 'areas of experience' identified by HMI in 1985 as a framework for curriculum design, which many Early Years educators have found more user-friendly than subjects, map well on to Gardner's intelligences.

Kieran Egan (1988) believes that we should turn the content of the curriculum for young children upside-down. He argues that a so-called child-centred curriculum in the United States, with its 'programmed reading schemes . . . and the absence of powerful emotional, dramatic or intellectual content', restricts them to a 'baby safe' learning diet characterized by 'Disneyesque sentimentality . . . the exact equivalent to intellectual contempt' (199). In his view young children's intellectual lives are most attuned to an oral culture – sounds rather than words – and introducing them to 'the technologies' of writing and reading too early, impoverishes their intellectual lives by forcing them to use tools for thinking which depress rather than enhance their reasoning powers. He believes that bi-polar opposites and grand universal concepts – good/evil, right/ wrong, big/small, hot/cold – should form the basis for curriculum design for young children and that stories should be used to foster their natural interest in universal human emotions – love, hate, anger, fear, jealousy.

Such visionary ideas are likely to be dismissed by many as 'barmy theory' in the climate of anti-intellectualism in the United Kingdom in the 1990s, but I have found teachers responding positively to 'blue sky' ideas. They are looking for a vision for themselves and the children. The promised five-year moratorium on changes from top-down initiatives may provide time and space for teachers themselves to try to make sense of what matters for the education of young children for the twenty-first century. Maybe someone will listen to them this time.

REFERENCES

Alexander, R., Woodhead, C. and Rose, J. (1992) *Curriculum Organisation and Classroom Practice in Primary Schools. A Discussion Paper.* London: DES.

Anning, A. and Billett, S. (1995) Four year olds in infant classes in small and large schools, in P. Broadhead (ed.) *BERA Dialogues.* Clevedon: Multi-lingual Matters.

Bennett, S.N. and Carré, C. (eds) (1993) *Learning to Teach.* London: Routledge.

Blyth, W.A.L. (1984) *Development, Experience and Curriculum in Primary Education.* Beckenham: Croom Helm.

Bowers, T. (1994) A Trying Time? *Special Children*, 75: 9–10.

Cleave, S. and Brown, S. (1989) *Meeting their Needs.* Windsor: NFER/Nelson.

Cleave, S. and Brown, S. (1991a) *Quality Matters.* Windsor: NFER/Nelson.

Cleave, S. and Brown, S. (1991b) *Four Year Olds in Infant Classes.* NFER/Nelson.

Dearing, R. (1993a) *The National Curriculum and its Assessment: An Interim Report.* London: SCAA.

Dearing, R. (1993b) *The National Curriculum and its Assessment: Final Report.* London: SCAA.

DFE (1992) *Choice and Diversity: A New Framework for Schools*, Education White Paper. London: HMSO.

DFE (1993a) *The Initial Training of Primary School Teachers: New Criteria for Course Approval.* Draft paper, circular 14/93. London: HMSO.

DFE (1994a) *Code of Practice on the Identification and Assessment of Special Educational Needs.* London: Central Office for Information.

DFE (1994b) *Special Educational Needs. A Guide for Parents.* London: Central Office for Information for the Department for Education.

DES (1985) *The Curriculum from 5 to 16: Curriculum Matters 2.* HMI Series. London: HMSO.

DES (1990) *Starting with Quality* (The Rumbold Report). London: HMSO.

DES (1991) *The Parent's Charter.* London: DES.

Egan, K. (1988) *Primary Understanding. Education in Early Childhood.* London: Routledge.

Galton, M. (1995) *Crisis in the Primary Classroom.* London: David Fulton Publishers.

Gardner, H. (1993a) *Multiple Intelligences: The Theory in Practice.* New York: Basic Books.

Gardner, H. (1993b) *The Unschooled Mind: How Children Think and How Schools Should Teach.* London: Fontana Press.

Hughes, M., Winkley, E. and Nash, T. (1994) *Parents and their Children's Schools.* Oxford: Basil Blackwell.

ILEA (1981) *The Early Years: A Curriculum for Young Children.* London: ILEA Centre for Learning Resources.

Kelly, A.V. (1994) A high-quality curriculum for the Early Years – some conceptual issues. *Early Years* (Journal of TACTYC), 15(1): 6–12.

Lewis, A. (1992) *Primary Special Needs and the National Curriculum.* London: Routledge.

Mittler, P. (1994) A post-code address in Platform. *Times Educational Supplement*, 13 May.

National Commission on Education (1993) *Learning to Succeed. A Radical Look at Education Today and A Strategy for the Future.* London: Heinemann.

SCAA (1994) *The Review of the National Curriculum. A Report on the 1994 Consultation.* London: SCAA.

Shulman, L. (1986) Those who understand: knowledge growth in teaching. *Educational Research*, 15: 4–14.

Summers, M. (1994) Science in the primary school: the problem of teachers' curricular expertise. *The Curriculum Journal*, 5(2): 179–94.

AUTHOR INDEX

SUBJECT INDEX